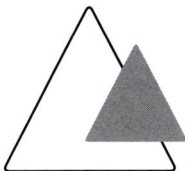

Contents

■ Units with this symbol are required for the Mathematics GCSE only.

NUMBER

ALGEBRA

Strand 1 Starting Algebra

Strand 2 Sequences

Strand 3 Functions and graphs

GEOMETRY AND MEASURES

Strand 1 Units and scales

Strand 2 Properties of shapes

Strand 3 Measuring shapes

Strand 4 Construction

FOU

Practice Book

MASTERING MATHEMATICS

FOR
WJEC GCSE

Practice • Reinforcement • Progress

Assessment Consultant and Editor: **Keith Pledger**

Keith Pledger, Gareth Cole, Joe Petran and Linda Mason

Series Editor: **Roger Porkess**

HODDER
EDUCATION
AN HACHETTE UK COMPANY

The publisher would like to thank the following for permission to reproduce copyright material:

Photo credits

p.111 © zuzule – Fotolia; **p.112t** © Syda Productions – Fotolia; **p.112b** © Stanislav Halcin – Fotolia.

Although every effort has been made to ensure that website addresses are correct at time of going to press, Hodder Education cannot be held responsible for the content of any website mentioned. It is sometimes possible to find a relocated web page by typing in the address of the home page for a website in the URL window of your browser.

Orders: please contact Bookpoint Ltd, 130 Milton Park, Abingdon, Oxon OX14 4SB. Telephone: (44) 01235 827720. Fax: (44) 01235 400454. Lines are open 9.00–17.00, Monday to Saturday, with a 24-hour message answering service. Visit our website at www.hoddereducation.co.uk.

© Keith Pledger, Gareth Cole, Joe Petran, Linda Mason 2016

First published in 2016 by

Hodder Education

An Hachette UK Company,

50 Victoria Embankment

London EC4Y 0DZ

Impression number	5	4	3	2	1
Year	2020	2019	2018	2017	2016

Cover photo © Sashkin - Fotolia

Illustrations by Integra

Typeset in India by Integra Software Services Pvt. Ltd., Pondicherry

Printed in Great Britain by CPI Group (UK) Ltd, Croydon CR0 4YY

A catalogue record for this title is available from the British Library.

ISBN 978 1471 874581

Strand 5 Transformations

Strand 6 Three-dimensional shapes

STATISTICS AND PROBABILITY

Strand 1 Statistical measures

Strand 2 Statistical diagrams

Strand 3 Collecting data

Strand 4 Probability

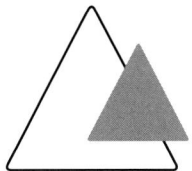

How to get the most from this book

Introduction

This book is part of the Mastering Mathematics for WJEC GCSE series and supports the textbook by providing lots of extra practice questions for the Foundation tier in Mathematics and Mathematics – Numeracy.

This Practice Book is structured to match the Foundation Student's Book and is likewise organised by key areas of the specification: Number, Algebra, Geometry & Measures and Statistics & Probability. Every chapter in this book accompanies its corresponding chapter from the textbook, with matching titles for ease of use.

Please note: the 'Moving On' units in the Student's Book cover prior knowledge only, so do not have accompanying chapters in this Practice Book. For this reason, although the running order of the Practice Book follows the Student's Book, you may notice that some Strand/Unit numbers appear to be missing, or do not start at '1'.

Progression through each chapter

Chapters include a range of questions that increase in difficulty as you progress through the exercise. There are three levels of difficulty across the Student's Books and Practice Books in this series. These are denoted by shaded spots on the right hand side of each page. Levels broadly reflect GCSE Maths grades as follows:

Low difficulty   GCSE Maths grades G–F

Medium difficulty   GCSE Maths grades F–E

High difficulty   GCSE Maths grades E–D

You might wish to start at the beginning of each chapter and work through so you can see how you are progressing.

Question types

There is also a range of question types included in each chapter, which are denoted by codes to the left hand side of the question or sub-question where they appear. These are examples of the types of question that you will need to practice in readiness for the GCSE Maths Foundation exam.

PS Practising skills

These questions are all about building and mastering the essential techniques that you need to succeed.

DF Developing fluency

These give you practice of using your skills for a variety of purposes and contexts, building your confidence to tackle any type of question.

PB Problem solving

These give practice of using your problem solving skills in order to tackle more demanding problems in the real world, in other subjects and within Maths itself.

Next to any question, including the above question types, you may also see the below code. This means that it is an exam-style question

ES Exam style

This question reflects the language, style and wording of a question that you might see in your GCSE Maths Foundation exam.

Answers

There are answers to every question within the book on our website.

Please visit: www.hoddereducation.co.uk/MasteringmathsforWJECGCSE

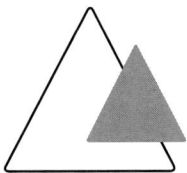

Number Strand 1 Calculating Unit 6 Multiplying and dividing negative numbers

| PS | PRACTISING SKILLS | DF | DEVELOPING FLUENCY | PB | PROBLEM SOLVING | ES | EXAM-STYLE |

PB **1** Work these out.

    a 5×-6

    b -2×-3

    c $-8 \div 2$

    d $-10 \div -5$

PB **2** Work these out.

    a $2\frac{1}{2} \times -2$

    b $-6 \div \frac{1}{2}$

    c $-8 \div -2$

    d $4\frac{1}{2} \times -4$

DF **3** Write down the two answers to each of these.

    a $\sqrt{25}$

    b $\sqrt{36} - 4$

    c $\sqrt{100} + 5$

DF **4** Write down the answer to each of these.

    a $(-5)^2$

    b $(-3)^2 - 4$

    c $(-4)^2 + 6$

PS **5** Use any two of the digits $-2, -3, 4, 6$ to make

    a the greatest product

    b the smallest difference

    c the smallest product.

PS **6** Write all the possible products using two of the digits –3, –2, 5, 7

ES **7** The temperature at midday was –4°C, by 9 p.m. the temperature had dropped to –9°C. By how many degrees Celsius (°C) did the temperature fall?

ES **8** At midday the temperature in Terreagle was:

–6°C on Monday

–3°C on Tuesday

3°C on Wednesday.

What was the mean temperature at midday for these three days?

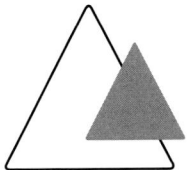

Number Strand 1 Calculating
Unit 7 BIDMAS

PS PRACTISING SKILLS   DF DEVELOPING FLUENCY   PB PROBLEM SOLVING   ES EXAM-STYLE

PS 1 Work these out.

   a $(8 + 6) \times 3$

   b $8 + 6 \times 3$

   c $8 + (6 \times 3)$

   d $(18 - 6) \div 3$

   e $18 - 6 \div 3$

   f $18 \div (6 - 3)$

PS 2 Work these out.

   a $17 - 9 \div 3$

   b $(18 - 9) \div 3$

   c $17 - (9 \div 3)$

   d $18 \div 9 - 3$

   e $18 + 9 \div 3$

   f $18 - (9 \div 3)$

DF 3 Find the value of $p^2 + (q + r)^2$ when

   a $p = 2, q = 3, r = 4$

   b $p = 3, q = 5, r = 7$

   c $p = 10, q = 2, r = 3$

   d $p = 5, q = 2, r = 3$

   e $p = 4, q = 5, r = 6$

   f $p = 10, q = 7, r = 3$

PS 4 Work these out.

   a $5 \times (2 + 8 \times 3^2)$

   b $(5 \times 2) + (8 \times 3^2)$

   c $5 \times (2 + 8) \times 3^2$

   d $5 \times (8 \div 2 \times 3^2)$

e $(8 \times 2) + (18 \div 3^2)$

f $5 \times (8 \div 2) \times 3^2$

PB **5** Penny takes a taxi which charges £2, plus £1 for every mile travelled. The driver charges £15 for a five mile journey. Penny says this is incorrect. Is she right? Explain your answer.

DF **6** Add brackets ( ) to make each statement correct.

   a $8 \times 7 + 6 \div 2 = 59$

   b $8 \times 7 + 6 \div 2 = 52$

   c $8 \times 7 + 6 \div 2 = 80$

   d $6 \times 7 + 8 \div 2^2 = 44$

   e $2^3 \times 2 + 10 \div 2 = 48$

   f $3^2 \times 3 + 18 \div 3^2 = 29$

PB **7** A Cash & Carry warehouse sells boxes of kitchen rolls.
Kitchen rolls cost £10 each for the first 12 boxes,
£7 each for the next 15 boxes,
and £5 for the next 20 boxes,
Barry wants to buy 36 boxes.
How much will he pay?

DF **8** Insert the correct symbols below to make these correct.

   a $3 \quad 3 \quad 3 \quad 3 = 36$

   b $3 \quad 3 \quad 3 \quad 3 = 10$

   c $3 \quad 3 \quad 3 \quad 3 = 3$

PB
ES **9** An electricity company charges a basic fee of £22.
The company also charges £3 during the daytime when the heating is on and £1.50 during the night-time when the heating is on.
An office is heated for 20 days and 10 nights.
How much will the electricity company charge?

PB **10** Some of the numbers below must be written as **indices** to make the sums correct. Which ones?

   a $32 + (22 \div 2) = 20$

   b $(32 + 32) \div (4 \times 22) = 4$

   c $102 + 23 + 33 = 150$

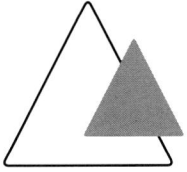

Number Strand 1 Calculating
Unit 8 Multiplying decimals

PS - PRACTISING SKILLS   DF - DEVELOPING FLUENCY   PB - PROBLEM SOLVING   ES - EXAM-STYLE

The questions in this unit should be answered *without* the use of a calculator.

PS 1 Find these.

    a 0.8×0.4

    b 0.7×0.8

    c 0.9×0.7

    d 32×0.04

    e 66×0.66

    f 127×0.005

    g $23 \times 0.6 \times 0.2$

    h $0.04 \times 0.5 \times 0.6$

    i $1250 \times 0.08 \times 0.02$

PS 2 Work out the cost of these.

    a 8 balloons at £1.23 each

    b 7 tickets at £22.75 each

    c 25 bracelets at £26.34 each

    d 12 packets of crisps at £0.55 each

    e 180 roof tiles at £2.42 each

    f 32 plants at £2.45 each

PS 3 You know that $27 \times 59 = 1593$. Use it to find these.

    a 2.7×5.9

    b 27×0.59

    c 270×0.59

    d 0.27×0.59

    e 2.7×0.0059

    f 0.027×0.0059

PB **ES** **4** Aled and Dewi are going to France. Aled exchanges £198 at an exchange rate of £1 = €1.39. Dewi exchanges £212 at an exchange rate of £1 = €1.37.

How many Euros (€) do they have in total?

DF **5** Find these.

a $5 \times (-0.3)$

b $0.5 \times (-0.3)$

c $(-0.5) \times (-0.3)$

d $7 \times (-2.4)$

e $(-2.7) \times (-2.3)$

f $(-127) \times (-0.115)$

DF **6** Gareth fills up his car at three different petrol stations during a week. At the first station he buys 29 litres of petrol at £1.35 per litre. At the second station he buys 27.2 litres of petrol at £1.30 per litre. At the third he buys 31.5 litres of petrol at £1.32 per litre.

How much does he pay in total?

PB **ES** **7** Use of a gym costs £4.45 per hour or £69.50 for a monthly membership. Nicola expects to use the gym for 1.5 hours per day for 9 days of each month.

Should she choose to pay by the hour or take up monthly membership? Show your working.

PB **ES** **8** A monkey sanctuary houses 35 monkeys. Each monkey costs £5.34 per day to feed, over 365 days of the year. The entry fee for the monkey sanctuary is £5.50. The sanctuary has 21 000 visitors per year.

Does the monkey sanctuary make enough money to feed the monkeys? You may use a calculator for this question.

PB **ES** **9** A window cleaner has to clean 130 windows in a tower block. Each window measures 50 cm by 70 cm. Cleaning fluid costs £1.58 to clean every 10 m².

How much will it cost the window cleaner to clean the 130 windows?

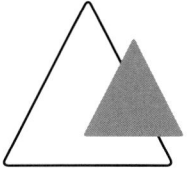

Number Strand 1 Calculating
Unit 9 Dividing decimals

PS — PRACTISING SKILLS   DF — DEVELOPING FLUENCY   PB — PROBLEM SOLVING   ES — EXAM-STYLE

PS **1** Work out these.

   a $2.18 \div 2$

   b $13.8 \div 3$

   c $21 \div 4$

   d $38 \div 8$

   e $66 \div 5$

   f $0.072 \div 6$

   g $23.125 \div 5$

   h $62 \div 8$

   i $39.168 \div 9$

PS **2** Work out the cost of one item in each of these.

   a 8 bottles of milk cost £6.24

   b 11 theatre tickets cost £313.50

   c 25 DVDs cost £246.25

   d 19 packets of peanuts cost £13.68

   e 180 light bulbs cost £277.20

   f 6 cars cost £53 970

PS **3** You know that $35 \div 5 = 7$. Use it to find these.

   a $3.5 \div 5$

   b $3.5 \div 0.5$

   c $350 \div 0.5$

   d $0.35 \div 5$

   e $3.5 \div 0.05$

   f $0.035 \div 0.005$

DF **4** Work out these.

 a $78 \div (-3)$

 b $(-61) \div 5$

 c $(-5.7) \div 3$

 d $2 \times 7 \div (-2.8)$

 e $54 \div (-2.7) \times (-2.3)$

 f $(-12) \times (-8.1) \div 3$

DF **5** Four people split a restaurant bill of £176.68 equally.
How much does each person pay?

DF **6** Marc buys some cheese which costs £2.56 per kilo. He pays £9.60.
How much cheese does he buy?

PB
ES **7** Work out these.

 a In one week, Alwen earned £279.50 for working 32.5 hours. Work
out Alwen's hourly rate of pay.

 b In the same week, Owain earned £315 for working 37.5 hours.
Work out Owain's hourly rate of pay.

PB
ES **8** In 2014, 12 people hire a coach at a cost of £319.80. Each pay
an equal share. In 2015, they hire the same coach which now
costs £337.20.
How much extra does each person pay in 2015?

PB
ES **9** Llinos bought a car for £9000. She paid a deposit of £1500 and
the rest in 24 equal payments.
How much was each repayment?

PB
ES **10** Kayleigh exchanges money in a bank for a holiday and receives
€310.08 for £228. Peter exchanges money in a post office and receives
€369.84 for £268.
Who gets the best deal?

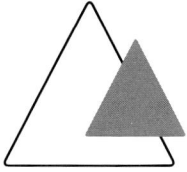

Number Strand 2 Using our number system Unit 5 Using the number system effectively

PS PRACTISING SKILLS   **DF** DEVELOPING FLUENCY   **PB** PROBLEM SOLVING   **ES** EXAM-STYLE

PS 1 Work these out.

a 8400×1000

b 8400×100

c 8400×10

d 8400×0.1

e 8400×0.01

f 8400×0.001

g 4978×1000

h 4978×100

i 4978×10

j 4978×0.1

k 4978×0.01

l 4978×0.001

PS 2 Work these out.

a 60×0.1

b 340×0.1

c 5400×0.01

d 2230×0.01

e 690×0.001

f 223×0.001

PS 3 Work these out.

    a 2.1×0.1

    b 6.25×0.1

    c 13.7×0.01

    d 245.6×0.01

    e 0.3×0.001

    f 4.57×0.001

PS 4 Work these out.

    a $2.1 \div 0.1$

    b $6.25 \div 0.1$

    c $13.7 \div 0.01$

    d $245.6 \div 0.01$

    e $0.3 \div 0.001$

    f $4.57 \div 0.001$

DF 5 Write the answers to these calculations in order of size, smallest first.

    a 4.8×0.1

    b $3.56 \div 0.1$

    c 29.8×0.01

    d $75.5 \div 0.01$

    e 19.9×0.001

    f $0.72 \div 0.001$

DF 6 Find the missing numbers.

    a $250 \times \square = 25$

    b $250 \div \square = 25$

    c $1.98 \times \square = 1980$

    d $1.98 \div \square = 1980$

    e $654 \times \square = 6.54$

    f $654 \div \square = 6.54$

PB **7** A game of mathematical 'snap' uses cards as shown below.
Use arrows to show which two cards are equal.

8.88 × 0.1	88.8 × 0.001	8.88 ÷ 0.1
a	**b**	**c**

8.88 ÷ 0.01	888 × 0.1	888 ÷ 0.1
d	**e**	**f**

PB **8** The signpost in Mathsland offers you four routes to your destination.
Which is the shortest?

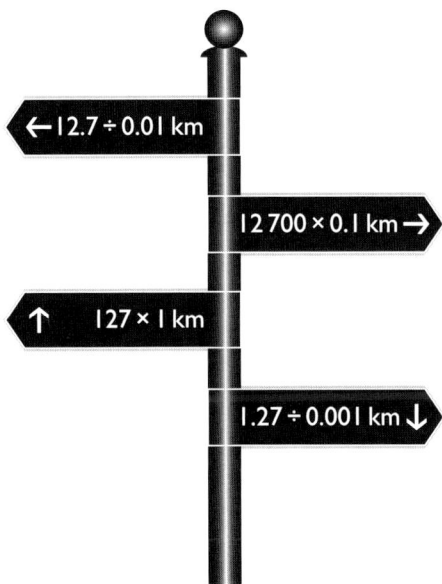

← 12.7 ÷ 0.01 km

12 700 × 0.1 km →

↑ 127 × 1 km

1.27 ÷ 0.001 km ↓

PB **9** Here are some calculations involving numbers.

2.56 × 100	2.56 ÷ 100	2.56 × 0.1

2.56 ÷ 0.001	2.56 × 0.001	2.56 ÷ 0.1

Arrange them in order of size from largest to smallest.

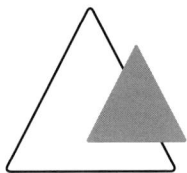

Number Strand 2 Using our number system Unit 6 Understanding standard form

PS — PRACTISING SKILLS   DF — DEVELOPING FLUENCY   PB — PROBLEM SOLVING   ES — EXAM-STYLE

PS 1 Write these numbers in standard form.

    a 847

    b 84 700

    c 0.000 847

    d 0.000 000 847

PS 2 Write these numbers in standard form.

    a 620

    b 820 000

    c 20 million

    d 1 millionth

PS 3 Write these as ordinary numbers.

    a 8.52×10^2

    b 3.4×10^{-3}

    c 2.02×10^5

    d 5.762×10^8

    e 4.55×10^{-7}

PS 4 Write these numbers in standard form.

    a 0.003 45

    b 0.000 005 48

    c 0.000 765 4

    d 0.000 000 234 5

DF **5** Write these numbers in standard form.

    a Eight thousand

    b Four fifths

    c Six hundredths

DF **6** Write these quantities in standard form.

    a The distance between the Earth and the Sun is 93 million miles.

    b The area of one person's skin is about $15000 \, cm^2$.

    c The distance from the equator to the north pole is 20000 km.

    d There are about 400 million stars in the Milky Way.

    e The area of the UK is $243610 \, km^2$.

DF **7** Write these numbers in order, starting with the smallest.

    a 4.2×10^{-3}

    b 7.21×10^{-2}

    c 0.09

    d 8.2×10^{-3}

    e 5.7×10^{2}

    f 3.6×10^{3}

    g 6.2×10^{2}

    h 0.57

PB **8** The table shows the distances of the Sun to nearby stars.

An astronomer is researching the stars and needs to make sure his list is in order, with the stars nearest to the Sun first. Show the list he needs to write.

Star	Distance from the Sun (in km)
Procyon B	1.08×10^{14}
Barnard's Star	5.67×10^{13}
Proxima Centauri	3.97×10^{13}
Sirius A	8.136×10^{13}
Ross 128	1.031×10^{14}
Wolf 359	7.285×10^{13}
Rigil Kentaurus	4.07×10^{13}
Luyten 726	7.95×10^{13}

Number Strand 3 Accuracy Unit 4 Rounding to 2 decimal places

PS ▸ PRACTISING SKILLS   **DF** ▸ DEVELOPING FLUENCY   **PB** ▸ PROBLEM SOLVING   **ES** ▸ EXAM-STYLE

The questions in this unit should be answered *without* the use of a calculator, unless otherwise specified.

PS **1** Round each of these numbers to two decimal places.   ●○○

    a 2.756

    b 12.462

    c 0.064

    d 0.896

    e 1.997

    f 65.507

    g 0.005

    h 9.995

    i 12.352

    j 10.002

PB **2** Ben buys a packet of seven identical pens for £1.99.   ●○○
Work out the cost of one pen. Give your answer to the nearest penny.

PB **3** You may use a calculator for this question   ●○○
Sylvia buys 35.6 litres of petrol at 123.9 pence per litre.
Work out the total cost of the petrol Sylvia bought.
Give your answer in pounds to the nearest penny.

DF **4** Work out the number which is halfway between   ●○○

    a 2.5 and 5.2

    b 0.23 and 0.24

    c 3.5 and 3.65

    d 2.05 and 2.049

    e 3.2 and 2.3

    f 6.25 and 6.255

g 10 and 10.001

h 7.98 and 8.003

DF **ES** **5** Here is a rectangle.

      a Work out the perimeter of the rectangle.
Give your answer to the nearest centimetre.

      b Work out the area of the rectangle.
Give your answer correct to one decimal place.

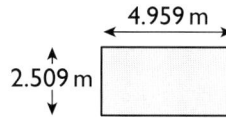

4.959 m

2.509 m

DF **ES** **6** Here is a regular hexagon. The length of one side 25.64 cm.

      a Work out the perimeter of the hexagon.
Give your answer correct to one decimal place.

      b Find the difference in the answer if you round
the length of each side before calculating
the perimeter with the answer you got for part **a**.

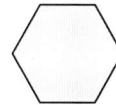

PB **ES** **7** Gwyn went fishing. He caught six fish. Here are the weights of
the fish he caught.

1.675 kg	2.420 kg	0.659 kg
2.093 kg	1.286 kg	3.450 kg

Find the mean weight of the fish he caught. Give your answer
correct to one decimal place.

DF **ES** **8** Here is a rectangle.

Explain why 12 cm² is not a sensible estimate for
the area of this rectangle.

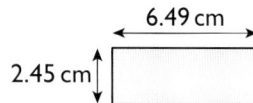

6.49 cm

2.45 cm

PB **ES** **9** Erica wants to know how many miles her car will travel using one
gallon of petrol.

She filled the petrol tank with petrol until it was full. She drove
her car for 307.6 miles. Erica then filled up her car's petrol tank
with 35.7 litres of petrol so it was full once again.

Work out how many miles Erica's car travelled using one gallon
of petrol. Give your answer correct to 2 decimal places.

1 gallon = 4.5461 litres

15

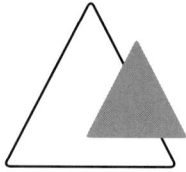

Number Strand 4 Fractions
Unit 3 Multiplying fractions

PS — PRACTISING SKILLS   DF — DEVELOPING FLUENCY   PB — PROBLEM SOLVING   ES — EXAM-STYLE

PS 1 Work out these.

   a $\dfrac{1}{2} \times \dfrac{1}{5}$

   b $\dfrac{1}{3} \times \dfrac{1}{7}$

   c $\dfrac{1}{2} \times \dfrac{3}{4}$

   d $\dfrac{1}{3} \times \dfrac{2}{5}$

   e $\dfrac{2}{3} \times \dfrac{4}{9}$

   f $\dfrac{3}{4} \times \dfrac{2}{7}$

   g $\dfrac{3}{4} \times \dfrac{3}{4}$

   h $\dfrac{5}{7} \times \dfrac{8}{9}$

PS 2 Work out these. Cancel the fractions before multiplying.

   a $\dfrac{1}{2} \times \dfrac{2}{3}$

   b $\dfrac{1}{4} \times \dfrac{8}{9}$

   c $\dfrac{1}{5} \times \dfrac{15}{16}$

   d $\dfrac{2}{3} \times \dfrac{6}{7}$

   e $\dfrac{3}{5} \times \dfrac{5}{8}$

   f $\dfrac{3}{4} \times \dfrac{4}{9}$

   g $\dfrac{5}{4} \times \dfrac{8}{15}$

   h $\dfrac{3}{7} \times \dfrac{14}{33}$

PS **3** Work out these. Cancel the fractions before multiplying.

a $\dfrac{1}{3} \times \dfrac{3}{5} \times \dfrac{5}{7}$

b $\dfrac{2}{5} \times \dfrac{6}{7} \times \dfrac{5}{6}$

c $\dfrac{4}{7} \times \dfrac{7}{8} \times \dfrac{3}{5}$

d $\dfrac{4}{9} \times \dfrac{5}{8} \times \dfrac{18}{25}$

e $\dfrac{9}{14} \times \dfrac{21}{25} \times \dfrac{5}{6}$

f $\dfrac{27}{72} \times \dfrac{64}{81} \times \dfrac{15}{16}$

DF **4** Match these cards.

half of $\frac{3}{8}$	$\frac{3}{8} \times \frac{2}{5}$	$\frac{3}{8}$ of $\frac{3}{4}$	$\frac{3}{4}$ of three quarters
a	**b**	**c**	**d**

$\frac{3}{4} \times \frac{2}{5}$	$\frac{1}{2} \times \frac{3}{8}$	$\frac{3}{8}$ of two fifths	$\frac{3}{4} \times \frac{3}{4}$
e	**f**	**g**	**h**

half of three quarters	three eighths of three quarters	$\frac{1}{2} \times \frac{3}{4}$	three quarters of $\frac{2}{5}$
i	**j**	**k**	**l**

DF **5** Complete these. Which symbol, <, > or = goes in each box?

a $\dfrac{4}{5} \times \dfrac{5}{7} \;\square\; \dfrac{4}{7}$

b $\dfrac{3}{5} \times \dfrac{5}{9} \;\square\; \dfrac{2}{3}$

c $\dfrac{2}{3} \times \dfrac{3}{4} \;\square\; \dfrac{1}{4}$

d $\dfrac{4}{7} \times \dfrac{7}{9} \;\square\; \dfrac{5}{9}$

e $\dfrac{15}{32} \times \dfrac{8}{25} \;\square\; \dfrac{3}{20}$

f $\dfrac{3}{4} \times \dfrac{8}{9} \;\square\; \dfrac{7}{8} \times \dfrac{4}{7}$

DF **6** Wilber has a stamp collection. He gives $\frac{3}{7}$ of his stamp collection

to Percy. Percy throws $\frac{1}{6}$ of these stamps away.

What fraction of Wilber's stamp collection did Percy throw away?

PB **7** Oliver gets an energy bill each year. Last year, $\frac{7}{12}$ of Oliver's energy

bill was for electricity. Oliver heats his water using electricity. $\frac{4}{5}$ of this
electricity was for heating water.

What fraction of Oliver's energy bill was for heating water?

DF **8** Complete these. What fraction goes in each box?

a $\frac{3}{7} \times \square = \frac{6}{35}$

b $\square \times \frac{2}{3} = \frac{8}{15}$

c $\frac{4}{5} \square = \frac{28}{45}$

d $\square \times \frac{5}{6} = \frac{5}{8}$

e $\frac{9}{10} \times \square = \frac{9}{14}$

f $\frac{3}{8} \times \square = \frac{1}{12}$

DF **9** Olwen cuts a piece of paper, A, into two parts, B and C.
She then cuts part C into two parts, D and E.

Part C is $\frac{1}{3}$ of part A. Part D is $\frac{3}{10}$ of part C.

What fraction of part A is

a part B

b part D

c part E?

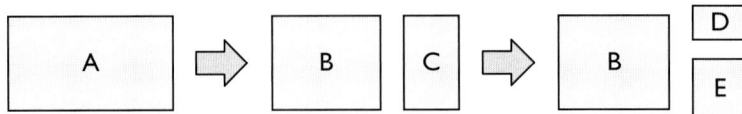

PB ES **10** Zebedee is given some money for his birthday. He spends $\frac{1}{4}$ of it
on music and $\frac{2}{3}$ of what is left on a pair of trousers.

What fraction of his birthday money did Zebedee spend on trousers?

PB
ES
11 At a pantomime, $\frac{5}{9}$ of the audience are children the rest are adults. $\frac{3}{5}$ of the children are boys. $\frac{2}{3}$ of the adults are females. What fraction of the audience are

a boys

b adult males?

PB
ES
12 Jake bought a car. At the end of the first year the value of the car was $\frac{3}{4}$ of its value at the beginning of the year. At the end of each following year, the value of the car was $\frac{8}{9}$ of its value at the beginning of that year.

Work out the smallest number of years for the car to more than halve its initial value.

DF **13** Work out the area of each of these shapes. Give your answers as fractions in their simplest form.

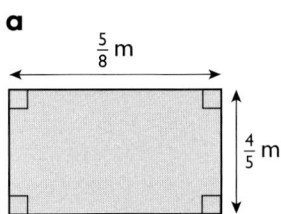

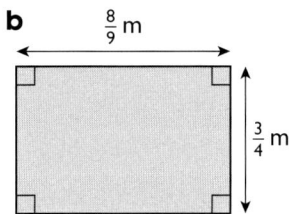

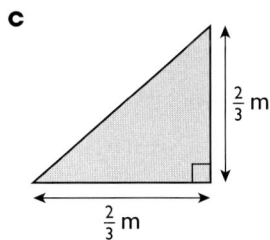

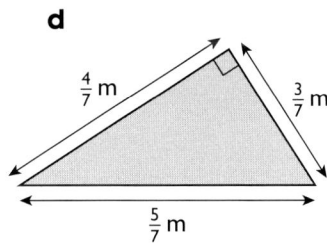

a

$\frac{5}{8}$ m

$\frac{4}{5}$ m

b

$\frac{8}{9}$ m

$\frac{3}{4}$ m

c

$\frac{2}{3}$ m

$\frac{2}{3}$ m

d

$\frac{4}{7}$ m

$\frac{3}{7}$ m

$\frac{5}{7}$ m

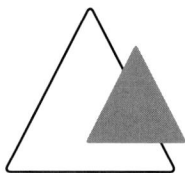

Number Strand 4 Fractions Unit 4 Adding and subtracting fractions

PS — PRACTISING SKILLS **DF** — DEVELOPING FLUENCY **PB** — PROBLEM SOLVING **ES** — EXAM-STYLE

PS **1** Work out these.

a $\dfrac{1}{5} + \dfrac{2}{5}$

b $\dfrac{4}{7} + \dfrac{2}{7}$

c $\dfrac{5}{9} - \dfrac{3}{9}$

d $\dfrac{13}{15} - \dfrac{2}{15}$

e $\dfrac{3}{20} + \dfrac{7}{20} + \dfrac{9}{20}$

f $\dfrac{5}{17} + \dfrac{8}{17} - \dfrac{3}{17}$

g $\dfrac{10}{13} - \dfrac{8}{13} + \dfrac{3}{13}$

h $\dfrac{9}{11} - \dfrac{3}{11} - \dfrac{5}{11}$

PS **2** Work out these.

a $1 - \dfrac{1}{6}$

b $1 - \dfrac{2}{7}$

c $1 - \dfrac{5}{8}$

d $1 - \dfrac{31}{100}$

e $1 - \dfrac{1}{10} - \dfrac{2}{10}$

f $1 - \dfrac{4}{11} - \dfrac{2}{11}$

g $1 - \dfrac{17}{21} + \dfrac{9}{21}$

h $1 - \dfrac{27}{35} + \dfrac{11}{35}$

PS **3** Work out these. Give your answers as fractions in their simplest form.   ● ○ ○

a $\dfrac{1}{8} + \dfrac{1}{4}$

b $\dfrac{3}{10} + \dfrac{1}{2}$

c $\dfrac{2}{3} + \dfrac{1}{9}$

d $\dfrac{3}{4} + \dfrac{1}{12}$

e $\dfrac{15}{16} - \dfrac{3}{4}$

f $\dfrac{4}{5} - \dfrac{7}{20}$

g $\dfrac{13}{18} - \dfrac{4}{9}$

h $\dfrac{7}{9} - \dfrac{4}{27}$

PS **4** Work out these. Give your answers as fractions in their simplest form.   ● ○ ○

a $\dfrac{1}{3} + \dfrac{1}{4}$

b $\dfrac{1}{4} + \dfrac{2}{7}$

c $\dfrac{3}{5} - \dfrac{1}{3}$

d $\dfrac{5}{7} - \dfrac{2}{3}$

e $\dfrac{3}{8} + \dfrac{2}{5}$

f $\dfrac{5}{6} - \dfrac{4}{7}$

g $\dfrac{3}{8} + \dfrac{5}{12}$

h $\dfrac{7}{9} - \dfrac{5}{12}$

DF **5** A bag contains only red, yellow and green counters. $\dfrac{2}{9}$ of the counters   ● ○ ○
are red. $\dfrac{3}{5}$ of the counters are yellow.

What fraction of the counters are

a   not red

b   red or yellow

c   green?

DF **6** $x = \dfrac{3}{5}, y = \dfrac{1}{7}$. Work out

   a $x + y$

   b $x - y$

   c $2x - 3y$.

DF **7** Complete these. What fraction goes in each box for the answer to be correct?

   a $\dfrac{3}{7} + \square = \dfrac{5}{7}$

   b $\dfrac{56}{99} - \square = \dfrac{27}{99}$

   c $\dfrac{7}{8} - \square = \dfrac{2}{5}$

   d $\dfrac{5}{16} + \square = \dfrac{7}{8}$

   e $\dfrac{5}{9} + \square = \dfrac{2}{3}$

   f $\dfrac{3}{8} + \square = \dfrac{7}{12}$

   g $\dfrac{4}{9} - \square = \dfrac{5}{12}$

   h $\dfrac{19}{27} - \square = \dfrac{7}{18}$

DF **8** Pierre is reading a book. He reads $\dfrac{1}{5}$ of the book on Friday, $\dfrac{1}{4}$ of the book on Saturday and $\dfrac{1}{3}$ of the book on Sunday.

What fraction of the book has he read all together?

DF **9** Work out these. Give your answers as fractions in their simplest form.

   a $1 - \left(\dfrac{5}{8} - \dfrac{2}{5} \right)$

   b $\left(\dfrac{5}{6} + \dfrac{1}{3} \right) - \left(\dfrac{5}{6} - \dfrac{1}{2} \right)$

   c $\left(\dfrac{3}{8} - \dfrac{1}{4} \right) + \left(\dfrac{4}{5} - \dfrac{3}{10} \right)$

PB
ES **10** The pie chart shows information about the different types of pizza some students like the best. $\dfrac{4}{11}$ of the students like ham and pineapple the best.

   a What fraction of the students like pepperoni the best?

   b What fraction of the students like cheese and tomato the best?

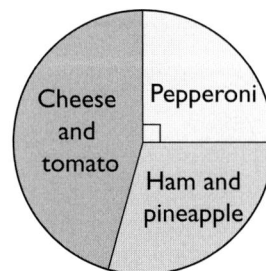

PB **ES** **11** Here are three paint pots, pot A, pot B and pot C. All three pots are the same size.

Pot A contains $\frac{1}{5}$ of a pot of paint. Pot B contains twice as much paint as pot A. Pot C contains $\frac{1}{4}$ of a pot of paint.

Jim wants to combine all the paint into one pot. Can he do it? Show how you get your answer.

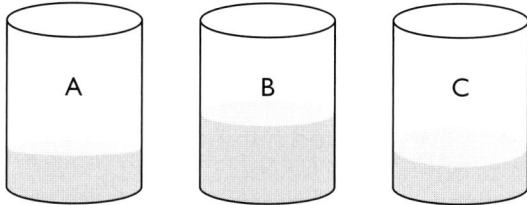

DF **ES** **12** The diagram shows a rectangle.
Work out the perimeter of the rectangle.
Give your answer as a fraction in its simplest form.

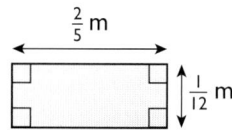

PB **ES** **13** Arwyn mixes lime cordial with water to make a glass of lime drink.

He uses $\frac{1}{20}$ of a bottle of lime cordial to make each glass of lime drink.
Arwyn has $\frac{5}{8}$ of a bottle of lime cordial. He wants to make as many glasses of lime drink as possible.

a How many glasses of the lime drink can he make?

b How much lime cordial does he have left?

PB **ES** **14** The volume of a piece of cheese is V cm³. Sarah cuts the piece of cheese into three parts. The volume of the smallest part is $\frac{1}{9}V$ cm³.
The volume of the largest is $\frac{3}{4}V$ cm³.

What is the volume of the remaining part? Give your answer in terms of V.

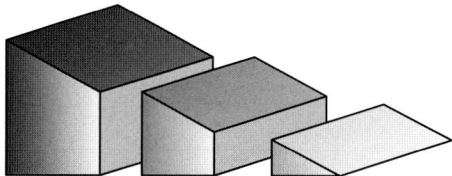

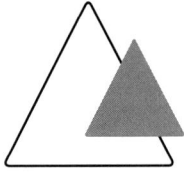

Number Strand 4 Fractions
Unit 5 Working with mixed numbers

PS — PRACTISING SKILLS   DF — DEVELOPING FLUENCY   PB — PROBLEM SOLVING   ES — EXAM-STYLE

PS **1** Copy and complete the table. Change between mixed numbers and top-heavy fractions. The first one has been done for you.

	a	b	c	d	e	f	g	h
Mixed number	$1\frac{3}{5}$	$2\frac{2}{3}$			$3\frac{4}{7}$	$7\frac{5}{6}$		$5\frac{7}{19}$
Top-heavy fraction	$\frac{8}{5}$		$\frac{13}{4}$	$\frac{39}{5}$			$\frac{131}{9}$	

PS **2** Work out these. Write each answer as a mixed number.

a $2\frac{2}{5} + \frac{4}{5}$

b $3\frac{4}{5} - 1\frac{1}{5}$

c $5\frac{5}{7} + 2\frac{4}{7}$

d $3\frac{2}{7} - 1\frac{3}{7}$

e $1\frac{3}{10} + 2\frac{2}{5}$

f $4\frac{1}{3} - 2\frac{2}{9}$

g $2\frac{5}{6} + 3\frac{7}{12}$

h $4\frac{2}{11} - 1\frac{9}{22}$

i $3\frac{7}{15} + 1\frac{13}{20}$

PS **3** Work out these. Write each answer as a mixed number.

a $1\frac{2}{3} + 1\frac{3}{4}$

b $3\frac{4}{5} - 1\frac{2}{3}$

c $4\frac{1}{4} - 2\frac{4}{5}$

d $3\frac{2}{5} + 1\frac{1}{6}$

e $1\frac{5}{6} + 2\frac{2}{7}$

f $3\frac{2}{9} + 2\frac{3}{5}$

g $3\frac{5}{7} - 1\frac{7}{9}$

h $5\frac{5}{12} - 2\frac{6}{15}$

i $3\frac{4}{15} + 5\frac{7}{45}$

PS **4** Work out these. Cancel the fractions before multiplying.

a $2\frac{2}{3} \times \frac{3}{4}$

b $\frac{3}{5} \times 3\frac{3}{4}$

c $1\frac{3}{5} \times 3\frac{1}{3}$

d $3\frac{1}{5} \times 1\frac{3}{4}$

e $1\frac{1}{5} \times 4\frac{1}{6}$

f $5\frac{1}{4} \times 2\frac{2}{7}$

g $3\frac{3}{5} \times \frac{8}{9}$

h $2\frac{2}{7} \times 4\frac{3}{8}$

i $4\frac{4}{9} \times 5\frac{5}{8}$

DF **5** Rhian has two oil drums, P and Q. P contains $5\frac{3}{4}$ gallons of oil. Q contains $3\frac{2}{5}$ gallons of oil.

a Work out the total amount of oil in the two oil drums.

b P contains more oil than Q. How much more?

DF **6** Bryn plays draughts. He can win, lose or draw each game he plays.

Last year, Bryn won $55\frac{3}{4}$% of his games and he lost $32\frac{5}{6}$% of his games.
What percentage of his games did he draw?

DF **7** Here are two rectangles. Work out

   a the area

   b the perimeter of each rectangle. Give your answers as mixed numbers in their simplest form.

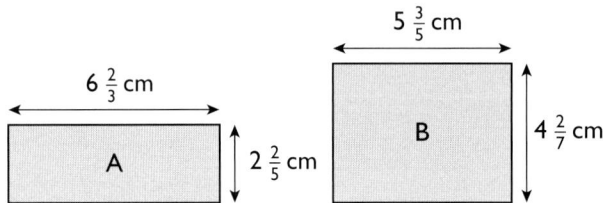

$5\frac{3}{5}$ cm

$6\frac{2}{3}$ cm

A

$2\frac{2}{5}$ cm

B

$4\frac{2}{7}$ cm

DF **8** In the triangle ABC, angle ABC = $61\frac{2}{5}°$ and angle BCA = $72\frac{2}{3}°$.
Work out the size of angle CAB.

PB
ES **9** Riley uses a lorry to take gravel to a building site. The table gives information about the amount of gravel Riley took to the building site each day last week.

Riley says: 'I took more than $12\frac{1}{2}$ tons of gravel to the building site

last week.' Is he right? Show how you get your answer.

Day	Monday	Tuesday	Wednesday	Thursday	Friday
Amount of gravel (in tons)	$2\frac{3}{4}$	2	$3\frac{1}{3}$	$1\frac{3}{5}$	3

PB
ES **10** Liam drives a car in California. On Saturday, he drove his car to see his sister. He used $\frac{2}{3}$ of a tank of petrol. On Sunday, Liam refilled the tank and drove his car to see his brother. He used $\frac{5}{6}$ of a tank of petrol. The petrol tank in Liam's car holds $7\frac{3}{5}$ gallons of petrol. He pays $2.80 for a gallon of petrol.

How much did Liam pay in total for the petrol he used to see his sister and brother?

PB **11** Here are two signposts on a footpath.

Work out the distance on the footpath between

a Stoneford and Upton

b the two sign posts

c Upton and Pen Hill.

Stoneford $3\frac{3}{5}$ Pen Hill $2\frac{1}{4}$ miles   Stoneford $1\frac{2}{3}$ Upton $1\frac{3}{4}$

PB **12** The diagram shows an empty room. The room is in the shape of a
ES cuboid. An extractor fan is used to filter the air in the room. It takes
the extractor fan 3 minutes 20 seconds to filter $2\,m^3$ of air.

Work out the shortest time it takes the extractor fan to filter all
the air in the room.

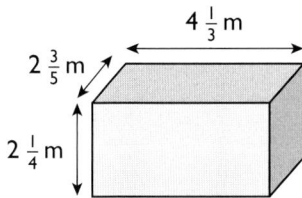

$4\frac{1}{3}$ m

$2\frac{3}{5}$ m

$2\frac{1}{4}$ m

DF **13** $A = 2\frac{4}{5}, B = 3\frac{4}{7}$. Work out

a $A + B$

b AB

c $5A + 7B$

d $5(B - A)$

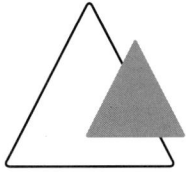

Number Strand 4 Fractions
Unit 6 Dividing fractions

PS — PRACTISING SKILLS   DF — DEVELOPING FLUENCY   PB — PROBLEM SOLVING   ES — EXAM-STYLE

The questions in this unit should be answered *without* the use of a calculator.

PS 1 Pair each number with its reciprocal.

$\frac{1}{2}$	5	$\frac{3}{10}$	$\frac{2}{5}$	$3\frac{1}{3}$
$\frac{4}{15}$	2	$2\frac{1}{2}$	$\frac{1}{5}$	$3\frac{3}{4}$

PS 2 Change each of these into a multiplication and then work out the answer.

a $5 \div \frac{1}{2}$

b $8 \div \frac{1}{3}$

c $9 \div \frac{1}{4}$

d $10 \div \frac{2}{3}$

e $15 \div \frac{3}{5}$

f $20 \div \frac{5}{7}$

g $\frac{3}{5} \div 4$

h $\frac{2}{3} \div 5$

i $\frac{4}{7} \div 8$

PS **3** Change each of these into a multiplication and then work out the answer. Cancel the fractions before multiplying.

a $\dfrac{7}{10} \div \dfrac{1}{5}$

b $\dfrac{3}{8} \div \dfrac{1}{4}$

c $\dfrac{5}{9} \div \dfrac{1}{3}$

d $\dfrac{9}{16} \div \dfrac{3}{4}$

e $\dfrac{9}{40} \div \dfrac{3}{5}$

f $\dfrac{8}{15} \div \dfrac{4}{5}$

g $\dfrac{5}{9} \div \dfrac{1}{6}$

h $\dfrac{7}{10} \div \dfrac{14}{15}$

i $\dfrac{15}{24} \div \dfrac{9}{16}$

PS **4** Change each of these into a multiplication and then work out the answer. Cancel the fractions before multiplying.

a $2\dfrac{1}{7} \div \dfrac{1}{7}$

b $5\dfrac{2}{3} \div \dfrac{1}{6}$

c $1\dfrac{5}{8} \div \dfrac{1}{4}$

d $\dfrac{3}{4} \div 1\dfrac{1}{8}$

e $\dfrac{8}{15} \div 1\dfrac{1}{5}$

f $\dfrac{5}{12} \div 2\dfrac{2}{9}$

g $3\dfrac{1}{9} \div 1\dfrac{1}{6}$

h $4\dfrac{9}{10} \div 1\dfrac{2}{5}$

i $7\dfrac{4}{7} \div 2\dfrac{2}{21}$

DF **5** A bag contains $1\dfrac{3}{5}$ lbs of sugar. A teaspoon holds $\dfrac{1}{150}$ lbs of sugar.

How many teaspoons of sugar are there in the bag?

DF **6** Which symbol, =, < or > goes in each box?

a $1\dfrac{5}{9} \div \dfrac{7}{12} \; \square \; 2\dfrac{1}{3}$

b $\dfrac{2}{9} \div 1\dfrac{5}{6} \; \square \; \dfrac{5}{33}$

c $5\dfrac{1}{4} \div 1\dfrac{3}{8} \; \square \; 4$

d $7\dfrac{3}{16} \div 1\dfrac{3}{4} \; \square \; 4\dfrac{1}{14}$

DF **7** Write the answers to these in order of size. Start with the lowest number.

$5\dfrac{1}{3} \div 1\dfrac{5}{6}$	$4\dfrac{2}{5} \div 1\dfrac{1}{10}$	$7\dfrac{7}{8} \div 2\dfrac{3}{4}$	$10\dfrac{5}{12} \div 3\dfrac{1}{6}$

DF **8** Complete this multiplication grid.

×	$1\dfrac{2}{5}$	**b**
$3\dfrac{3}{4}$	**a**	$2\dfrac{1}{4}$
c	**d**	$5\dfrac{2}{3}$

DF **9** Work out these.

a $2\dfrac{1}{3} \times 3\dfrac{3}{7} \div 2\dfrac{4}{9}$

b $5\dfrac{3}{4} \div 2\dfrac{5}{8} \times 3\dfrac{1}{2}$

c $8\dfrac{2}{5} \div 2\dfrac{7}{10} \div 1\dfrac{4}{9}$

PB **ES** **10** The diagram shows a rectangular wall.

The area of the wall is $5\dfrac{5}{9}$ m².

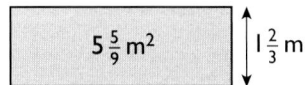

The width of the wall is $1\dfrac{2}{3}$ m.

Work out the perimeter of the wall.

$5\tfrac{5}{9}$ m² $1\tfrac{2}{3}$ m

PB
ES
11 Oleg has two boxes of soap powder. The soap powder is the same type in each box. Oleg puts the soap powder from these boxes into bags. Each bag contains $\frac{2}{5}$ kg of soap powder when full. He fills as many bags as possible.

On Saturday, Oleg sells all the bags of soap powder at a market.
He makes 75p profit on each bag of soap powder he sells.
How much profit did Oleg make in total?

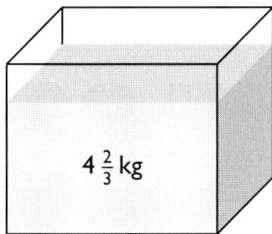
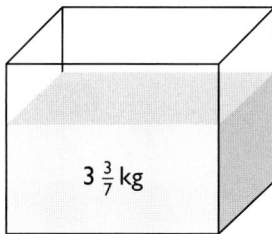

$4\frac{2}{3}$ kg $3\frac{3}{7}$ kg

PB
ES
12 Ravi is going to put some lawn feed on his lawn. The total area of Ravi's lawn is 125 m². A packet of lawn feed covers $4\frac{5}{7}$ m² of lawn.

Each packet of lawn feed costs £1.89. Ravi thinks he can cover his lawn with lawn feed for less than £50.
Is Ravi right? Show how you get your answer.

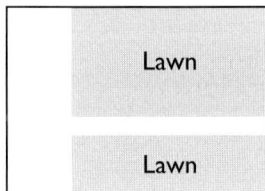

Lawn

Lawn

31

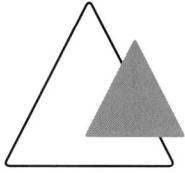

Number Strand 5 Percentages Unit 2 Calculate percentages of quantities with and without a calculator

PS — PRACTISING SKILLS   DF — DEVELOPING FLUENCY   PB — PROBLEM SOLVING   ES — EXAM-STYLE

PB **1** Answer these questions without using a calculator.

    a 10% of £340

    b 5% of £200

    c 25% of 400 metres

PB **2** Answer these questions without using a calculator.

    a 99% of £400

    b 3% of 500 metres

    c 14% of £500

DF **3** Harri used 26% of his full tank of petrol on Monday. His petrol tank holds 46 litres of fuel when full. Petrol costs £1.10 per litre.

    How much did the petrol cost that Harri used on Monday?
Give your answer to the nearest penny.

DF **4** Rowena is saving to buy a car that costs £4000. She has already saved 35% of the money she needs.

    How much more money does Rowena need to save to buy the car she wants?

PS **5** Dewi has an income of £19 000 per annum. He saves 20% of his income, he uses 35% to pay his rent, he spends 15% on food and entertainment. All the rest of his income goes on paying bills.

    How much per month does Dewi have to pay his bills?

PS **6** Bethan is offered a £2000 loan from *Llewun*. *Llewun* offers payments of £60 per month for 3 years. Bethan thinks she will pay 8% interest on this loan.

    Is she correct? You must show your working.

ES **7** Gwilym is offered a bonus of 6% of his £18 000 p.a. salary or £1000.
Which of these two options would give Gwilym the best bonus?
You must show all your working.

ES **8** Jodi pays 20% tax on the first £5000 she earns. Then she has to pay
45% tax on all the rest of the money she earns. Jodi earns £18 500 p.a.
How much tax will Jodi pay?

33

Number Strand 5 Percentages
Unit 3 Converting fractions and decimals to and from percentages

PS PRACTISING SKILLS   **DF** DEVELOPING FLUENCY   **PB** PROBLEM SOLVING   **ES** EXAM-STYLE

PS **1** Write these decimals as percentages.

  a 0.75

  b 0.25

  c 0.4

  d 0.38

  e 0.98

  f 0.165

  g 0.592

  h 0.06

PS **2** Write these percentages as decimals.

  a 75%

  b 18%

  c 90%

  d 5%

  e 29.5%

  f 7.4%

  g 156%

  h 0.14%

PS **3** Write these percentages as fractions in their simplest form.

  a 17%

  b 31%

  c 70%

  d 25%

e   20%

f   65%

g   72%

h   17.5%

PS **4** Write each fraction as a percentage.

a $\dfrac{41}{100}$

b $\dfrac{3}{10}$

c $\dfrac{4}{5}$

d $\dfrac{9}{20}$

e $\dfrac{17}{25}$

f $\dfrac{5}{8}$

g $\dfrac{9}{24}$

h $\dfrac{10}{32}$

DF **5** Write down, with reasons, which of these statements are true and which are false.

a $\dfrac{2}{5}$ is greater than 35%.

b   28% is equal to 0.28.

c $\dfrac{7}{9}$ is less than 75%.

d   0.65 is equal to $\dfrac{13}{20}$.

e $\dfrac{14}{35}$ is greater than 40%.

f   60% is less than $\dfrac{35}{56}$.

DF **6** A bag contains 50 counters. 27 of the counters are blue the rest are red.

a   What fraction of the counters are blue?

b   What percentage of the counters are blue?

c   What percentage of the counters are red?

DF **7** Gwen and Aled each took a language test. Gwen got 17 out of 20 in her Spanish test. Aled got 13 out of 15 in his French test.

Who got the higher percentage in their language test, Gwen or Aled?

DF **8** A weather forecaster says: 'There is an 85% probability of rain tomorrow.'

   a Write 85% as a decimal.

   b Write 85% as a fraction in its simplest form.

DF **9** The area of shape A is 54 cm². The area of shape B is 85 cm².

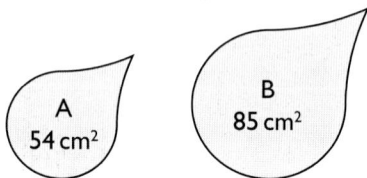

A
54 cm²

B
85 cm²

   a Work out the area of shape A as a percentage of the area of shape B.

   b Work out the area of shape B as a percentage of the area of shape A.

Give your answers to two decimal places.

DF **10** Henry saves coins in a jar. The diagram shows information about the coins in the jar.

   a How many coins are there in the jar?

   b What fraction of the coins are 20p coins?

   c What percentage of the coins are 10p coins?

   d Henry thinks that 35% of the coins are 5p coins. Is he right? Explain your answer.

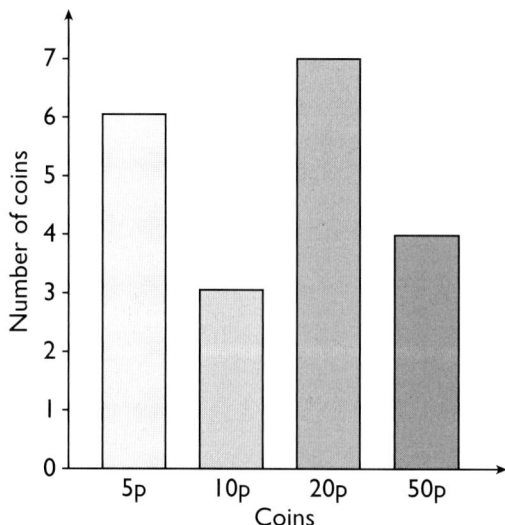

DF **11** Work out the missing entries in the table.

Fraction	Decimal	Percentage
$\frac{2}{3}$	$0.\dot{6}$	**a**
$\frac{4}{9}$	**b**	$44.\dot{4}\%$
c	$0.\dot{3}$	$33.\dot{3}\%$
$\frac{5}{11}$	$0.\dot{4}\dot{5}$	**d**
$\frac{7}{22}$	**e**	$31.8\dot{1}\%$

DF **12** Write $\frac{7}{20}$, 40%, 0.3 and $\frac{11}{25}$ in order of size. Start with the smallest.

PB **13** Akemi plays tennis. She can win, lose or draw the games she plays.

ES   Last year Akemi won 68% and lost $\frac{2}{7}$ of the games she played.

What percentage of the games did she draw? Give your answer correct to 2 decimal places.

PB **14** Which is greater $\frac{1}{3}$ or 30%? Give a reason for your answer.

ES

PB **15** Sioned grows pink tulips, red tulips and white tulips. She says: '25%

ES   of my tulips are pink, $\frac{9}{20}$ of my tulips are red and 0.35 of my tulips are white.'

Sioned cannot be correct. Explain why.

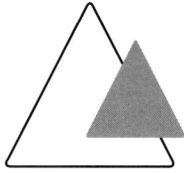

Number Strand 5 Percentages Unit 4 Applying percentage increases and decreases to amounts

PS — PRACTISING SKILLS   DF — DEVELOPING FLUENCY   PB — PROBLEM SOLVING   ES — EXAM-STYLE

PS **1** Work out these.
- **a i** 1% of £250
- **ii** 12% of £250
- **iii** Decrease £250 by 12%.

- **b i** 1% of £21.50
- **ii** 18% of £21.50
- **iii** Decrease £21.50 by 18%.

PS **2** Work out these.
- **a** Decrease 350 g by 17%.
- **b** Increase 326 m by 21%.
- **c** Decrease £24.50 by 6%.
- **d** Increase 560 *l* by 12.5%.
- **e** Decrease 125 cm by 7.5%.
- **f** Increase $1250 by 3.5%.

PS **3** Kim buys a power drill for £68.50 plus VAT at 20%.
How much does she pay?

PS **4** Jose buys a plate for £24. He sells it the next day for a profit of 45%.
How much does Jose sell the plate for?

DF **5** Complete these. Which symbol, <, > or = goes in each box?
- **a** £350 increased by 10% ☐ £430 decreased by 10%
- **b** $49.50 decreased by 15% ☐ $52.40 decreased by 20%
- **c** €128 increased by 29% ☐ €132 increased by 26%
- **d** ₳1250 decreased by 15.8% ☐ ₳1100 increased by 7.5%

DF **6** Ravi travels to work by train. On Monday it took him 1 hour 40 minutes to travel to work. On Tuesday it took him 15% less time to travel to work. How long did it take Ravi to travel to work on Tuesday?

DF **7** Yasmin has a meal at a restaurant. Here is her bill.

```
        Alf's Chip Shop
  Fish and chips      £9.85
  Tea                 £1.35
  Subtotal a
  15% service charge b
  Total to pay c
```

Work out the missing entries in the bill.

PB **ES** **8** The table gives information about the population of Riverton in 2005 and in 2015.

Marco says: 'The population of Riverton has increased by 10% from 2005 to 2015.' Is he right? Explain your answer.

Year	2005	2015
Population	15310	16678

PB **ES** **9** Fiona works in a warehouse. For the first 20 hours she works in a week she is paid at an hourly rate of £7.80. For each additional hour she works her hourly rate is increased by 35%. Last week Fiona worked 28 hours. Work out her pay.

PB **ES** **10** Morgan measures the lifetimes of two batteries, battery A and battery B. The lifetime of battery A was 36 hours. The lifetime of battery B was 48 hours. The manufacturer of the batteries claims that battery B lasts at least 30% longer than battery A.

Is the manufacturer correct? Explain your answer.

DF **ES** **11** Chelsea invests £4800 at 2.4% per annum simple interest. Work out the total value of the investment after 3 years.

PB **ES** **12** In the triangle ABC, angle CAB = 40° and angle ABC is 65% larger than angle CAB.

Work out angle BCA.

PB **13** The diagram shows two circles, circle P and circle Q. The area of circle P is 50 cm². The area of circle Q is 27.5% larger than the area of circle P.

Work out the radius of circle Q. Give your answer correct to 2 decimal places.

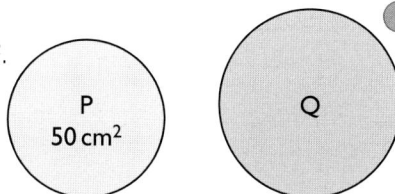

P
50 cm²

Q

Number Strand 5 Percentages Unit 5 Finding the percentage change from one amount to another

PS — PRACTISING SKILLS   **DF** — DEVELOPING FLUENCY   **PB** — PROBLEM SOLVING   **ES** — EXAM-STYLE

PS **1** Work out these.

   a Write £2.75 as a percentage of £20.

   b Write 49.5°C as a percentage of 112.5°C.

   c Write 720 mm as a percentage of 960 mm.

   d Write 15.6 *l* as a percentage of 32.5 *l*.

   e Write 45° as a percentage of 360°.

   f Write 49.5 s as a percentage of 120 s.

PS **2** Write the first number as a percentage of the second number.
Give each answer correct to 1 decimal place.

   a 2, 7

   b 17, 35

   c 27, 95

   d 29, 316

   e 359, 511

   f 511, 359

   g 18, 10.6

   h 0.789, 1.249

DF **3** Owen bought a car for £2400. The next day he sold the car for £3200.

   a How much profit did he make?

   b What is his percentage profit?

DF **4** Liam weighed 85 kg at the beginning of his diet and 77 kg at the end of his diet.

    a How much weight did he lose?

    b What is the percentage loss in his weight? Give your answer correct to 1 decimal place.

DF **5** The height of a tree at the beginning of the year is 17.5 m. The height of the tree at the end of the year is 18.9 m.

    Work out the percentage increase in the height of the tree.

PB **6** The diagram shows information about the counters in a bag.

ES   **a** Work out the percentage of blue counters in the bag.

    The percentage of black counters in the bag is greater than the percentage of green counters in the bag.

    b How much greater?

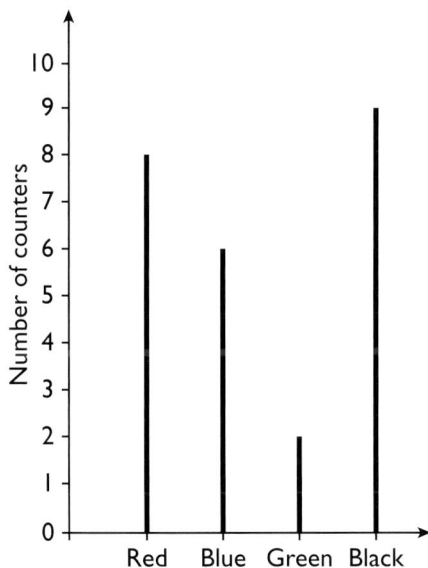

PB **7** A village collects £13 109 to build a new playground.

ES   The target is £20 000. The village magazine says: 'We've collected over 65% of our target, well done!'

    Is the village magazine right? Explain your answer.

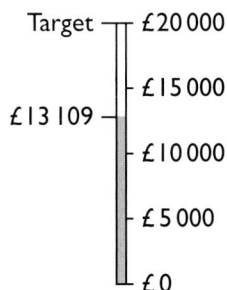

41

PB **8** The diagram gives information about the finances of a company.

ES **a** What percentage of the company's finances is taxes?

The company director gets a bonus if the profit is 10% greater than the costs.

b Does the company director get a bonus? Give a reason for your answer.

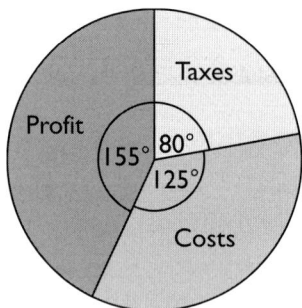

PB **9** A box contains only arrow shapes and star shapes.

ES **a** What percentage of the shapes are star shapes?

Ben is going to add some more arrow shapes to the box. He wants the percentage of arrow shapes in the box to equal 70%.

b How many more arrow shapes does he need to add to the box?

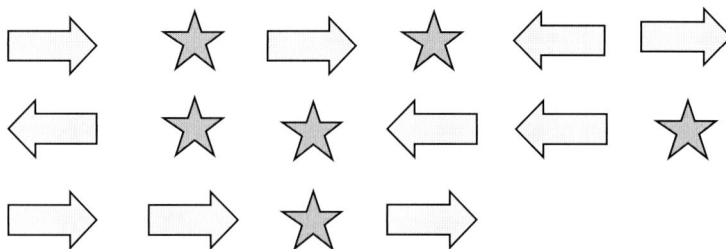

PB **10** The diagram shows the distances, in km, between some towns.

ES Laura is going to drive from Templeton to Tollercombe. The north route takes her through Whitchurch and Green Hill. The south route takes her through Thursk.

Work out the percentage increase in the length of her drive if she takes the north route rather than the south route. Give your answer correct to 1 decimal place.

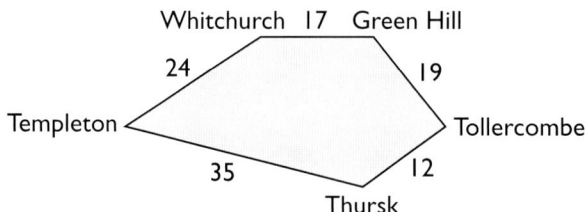

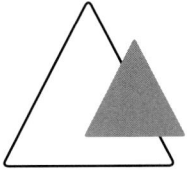

Number Strand 6 Ratio and proportion Unit 2 Sharing in a given ratio

PS — PRACTISING SKILLS **DF** — DEVELOPING FLUENCY **PB** — PROBLEM SOLVING **ES** — EXAM-STYLE

PS **1** Work these out.

    a Share 72 in the ratio 1:5.

    b Share 48 in the ratio 1:3.

    c Share 81 in the ratio 2:1.

    d Share 200 in the ratio 4:1.

PS **2** Work these out.

    a Share 60 in the ratio 2:3.

    b Share 91 in the ratio 3:4.

    c Share 105 in the ratio 5:2.

    d Share 250 in the ratio 7:3

PS **3** Work these out.

    a Share 54 in the ratio 1:3:2.

    b Share 90 in the ratio 5:2:3.

    c Share 117 in the ratio 2:3:4.

    d Share 425 in the ratio 1:1:3.

DF **4** Orange drink is made from orange concentrate and water in the ratio 1:14. Shelly makes some orange drink. She uses 25 ml of orange concentrate.

How much water does she need?

DF **5** A box of chocolates contains milk chocolates and plain chocolates in the ratio 3:4.

What fraction of the box of chocolates are

    a milk chocolates

    b plain chocolates?

DF **6** Haan and Ben win first prize in a tennis doubles competition.
The first prize is £600. They share the prize in the ratio 7:5.

a How much does Haan get?

Haan now shares his part of the prize with Tania in the ratio 2:3

b How much does Tania get?

DF **7** Gwen and Ellis share the cost of a meal in the ratio 2:5. The cost
of the meal is £66.50. Ellis pays more than Gwen.

How much more?

DF **8** A bag contains 20p coins and 50p coins in the ratio 7:5. There are
a total of 180 coins in the bag.

Work out the total amount of money in the bag.

DF **9** The area of pentagon A and
the area of pentagon B are in
the ratio 5:9. The area of
pentagon A is 105 cm².

Work out the area of
pentagon B.

A
105 cm²

B

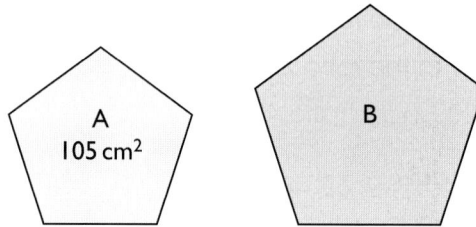

PB
ES **10** A box contains red, blue and green counters in the ratio 2:4:3.

a What fraction of the counters are blue?

b What fraction of the counters are not red?

There are 27 green counters in the bag.

c Work out the total number of counters in the bag.

PB
ES **11** Viki buys wooden chairs and plastic chairs in the ratio 3:7. The cost of
each wooden chair is £31.60. The cost of each plastic chair is £15.80.
The total cost of the wooden chairs is £284.40.

How much does Viki pay in total for the plastic chairs?

PB
ES **12** The angles in a triangle are in the ratio 2:3:7.

Show that the triangle is not a right-angled triangle.

PB **13** A box contains only blue pens and black pens in the ratio 5:4. Olivia
takes 8 blue pens from the box. The number of blue pens in the box is
now equal to the number of black pens in the box.

Work out the total number of pens in the box.

PB **14** The length and the width of a rectangle are in the ratio 5:3. The
perimeter of the rectangle is 120 cm.

Work out the area of the rectangle.

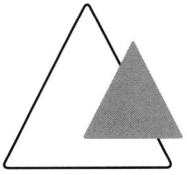

Number Strand 6 Ratio and proportion Unit 3 Working with proportional quantities

| PS | PRACTISING SKILLS | DF | DEVELOPING FLUENCY | PB | PROBLEM SOLVING | ES | EXAM-STYLE |

PS 1 Seven batteries cost a total of £8.75.

    a How much does 1 battery cost?

    b How much do 5 batteries cost?

PS 2 Twelve stamps cost a total of £6.96.

    a How much does 1 stamp cost?

    b How much do 17 stamps cost?

PS 3 Eight calculators cost a total of £46.80.

    a How much do 5 calculators cost?

    b How much do 13 calculators cost?

PS 4 There are a total of 252 matches in 7 identical boxes of matches. How many matches are there in

    a 5 boxes of matches

    b 11 boxes of matches?

PS 5 There are 180 packets of crisps in 5 boxes. How many packets of crisps are there in

    a 3 boxes

    b 8 boxes?

DF 6 Here is a recipe to make 12 almond shortbread biscuits. Grandma is going to use this recipe to make 21 biscuits. How much does she need of each ingredient?

```
            Almond shortbread biscuits
    (makes 12 biscuits)
    5oz butter              8oz flour
    1oz ground almonds      3oz caster sugar
```

DF **7** The label on a 0.75 *l* bottle of Fruit Squash says it makes 60 drinks.
What should the label on a 1.75 *l* bottle of Fruit Squash say about
the number of drinks it makes?

DF **8** Boxes of paperclips come in two sizes and prices.

    a For the small box of paperclips, work out the cost of 1 paperclip.

    b Which box is the better value for money? Explain your answer.

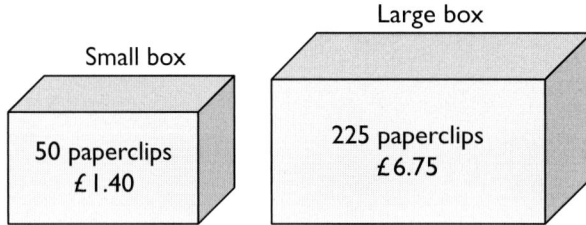

Large box

Small box

50 paperclips
£1.40

225 paperclips
£6.75

DF **9** For each of these, find the better value for money.
Explain your answers.

    a 5 rulers for £8 *or* 7 rulers for £10.50

    b 15 protractors for £10.20 *or* 12 protractors for £8.40

    c 13 compasses for £51 *or* 17 compasses for £66

DF **10** A spring stretches 6.3 cm when a force of 28 newtons (28 N) is applied to it.

    a How much will the spring stretch when a force of 15 N is
applied to it?

The spring stretches 2.7 cm when a force F N is applied to it.

    b Work out the value of F.

PB
ES **11** The table gives information about Mani's pay for last week.
This week Mani worked 30 hours at a standard rate and 10 hours
at a bonus rate.

How much more did he earn this week compared with last week?

	Number of hours worked	Total
Standard rate	35	£273.70
Bonus rate	5	£60.80
		£334.50

PB **ES** **12** Aabish is going to make some concrete. She has 100 kg of cement, 180 kg of sharp sand, 400 kg of aggregate and an unlimited supply of water.

Work out the greatest amount of concrete Aabish can make.

Materials for concrete	
(makes 0.125 m³)	
Cement	40 kg
Sharp sand	75 kg
Aggregate	150 kg
Water	22 l

PB **ES** **13** A parcel contains 12 large pies and 5 small pies. The total weight of the 12 large pies is 14.88 kg. The total weight of the 5 small pies is 4.25 kg.

John makes a different parcel. The parcel contains 8 large pies and 7 small pies.

a Work out the total weight of John's pies.

Jenny also makes a parcel. The parcel contains 7 large pies and some small pies. The total weight of all the pies in her parcel is 11.23 kg.

b Work out the number of small pies in Jenny's parcel.

PB **ES** **14** Baked beans come in three sizes of can. The table gives information about these cans.

Which size of can is the better value for money? Explain your answer.

Size of can	Weight of baked beans (grams)	Cost (p)
Small	180	28
Medium	415	64
Large	840	130

PB **15** The height of the Statue of Liberty is 305 feet. The height of St. Paul's Cathedral is 111 metres. (10 feet is approximately 3 metres)

Which is taller, the Statue of Liberty or St. Paul's Cathedral?

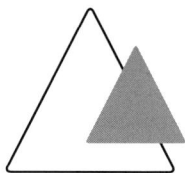

Number Strand 7 Number properties Unit 4 Index notation

PS — PRACTISING SKILLS   DF — DEVELOPING FLUENCY   PB — PROBLEM SOLVING   ES — EXAM-STYLE

PB **1** Write each of these as a power of 5.

    a $5 \times 5 \times 5$

    b $5 \times 5 \times 5 \times 5 \times 5 \times 5 \times 5$

PB **2** Write each of these in index form.

    a $7 \times 7 \times 7 \times 7$

    b $11 \times 11 \times 11$

DF **3** Write each of these using a single index.

    a $(5^2)^3$

    b $3^{10} \div 3^3$

    c $5^2 \times 5^7 \div 5^3$

DF **4** Write each of these in index form.

    a $2 \times 2 \times 5 \times 2 \times 5 \times 2 \times 2$

    b $3 \times 3 \times 5 \times 5 \times 3 \times 3 \times 5 \times 5$

PS **5** Given that $x = 2^4 \times 3^5$ and $y = 2^6 \times 3^2$, write xy in index form.

PS **6** $x = 2^3 \times 4^3$ and $x = 2^n$

    Find the value of n.

ES **7** Evaluate $2^3 \times 3^2$.

ES **8** Complete the statement.

    $5^6 \div 5^2 = 5^{\square}$

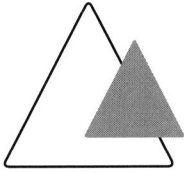

Number Strand 7 Number properties Unit 5 Prime factorisation

PS — PRACTISING SKILLS   DF — DEVELOPING FLUENCY   PB — PROBLEM SOLVING   ES — EXAM-STYLE

PB **1** Evaluate each of these.

    a $2 \times 2 \times 2 \times 3 \times 3 \times 5$

    b $3 \times 3 \times 3 \times 5$

PB **2** Write each of these numbers as a product of its prime factors in index form.

    a 80

    b 120

    c 400

PS **3** Work out the value of x, y and z.

    a $2^3 \times 2^x \times 5^2 = 1800$

    b $3^5 \times 2^y \times 7^2 = 1\,488\,375$

DF **4** Write the following as a product of prime factors in index form.

    a 1250

    b 2300

    c 21 609

PS **5** Gwen and Megan cycle around a race track. Each lap takes Gwen 45 seconds. Each lap takes Megan 50 seconds. Gwen and Megan start cycling together at the start line.

    How many laps behind Gwen will Megan be when they are both again together at the start line? You must show your working.

PS **6** Write 4 million using products of prime factors and index form.

ES **7** What is the smallest number that $2^3 \times 3^5 \times 7$ must be multiplied by to give a square number?

ES **8** Explain, using products of prime factors in index notation, why 300 is not a square number. You must show your working.

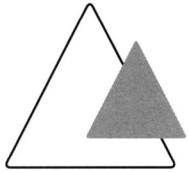

Algebra Strand 1 Starting Algebra Unit 4 Working with formulae

PS — PRACTISING SKILLS   DF — DEVELOPING FLUENCY   PB — PROBLEM SOLVING   ES — EXAM-STYLE

PS 1 Copy and complete the table for this number machine.

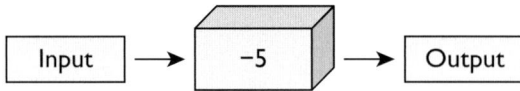

Input → -5 → Output

	Input	Output
a	20	
b		12
c	2	
d		−7
e	n	
f		p

PS 2 Copy and complete the table for this number machine.

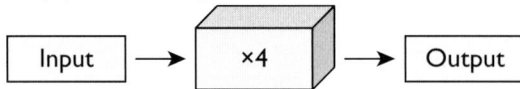

Input → $\times 4$ → Output

	Input	Output
a	3	
b		56
c	0.5	
d		17
e	m	
f		q

DF **3** Angus thinks of a number. He multiplies the number by 5.
He then adds 3.

   a Work out the result if the number Angus thought of was

     i 2

     ii 10

     iii n.

   b Work out the number Angus thought of when the result was

     i 38

     ii 3

     iii p.

DF **PB** **ES** **4** £1 = €1.40 and £1 = $1.60 are the exchange rates for the euro and
the US dollar to pounds.

   a Change

     i £50 to euros

     ii $50 to pounds

     iii €50 to US dollars.

   b A pair of sunglasses in Dublin cost €24.50. The same pair of
sunglasses in Florida cost $30. Work out the difference in the
cost of these sunglasses.

DF **5** Here is a rule to change a quantity in litres into a quantity in pints.

> Multiply the number of litres by 1.75 to get the number of pints.

   a Change 40 litres to pints.

   b Change 1050 gallons to litres. 1 gallon = 8 pints.

DF **PB** **ES** **6** $A = \dfrac{bh}{2}$ is the formula to find the area of a triangle, where the base is b
and the perpendicular height is h.

   a **i** Find A when $b = 5$ and $h = 7$.

     ii Find b when $A = 54$ and $h = 9$.

   b The area of a square is the same as the area of a triangle of
base 25 and height 8. What is the length of each side of
the square?

PB
ES

7 Fflur hires a car. The cost £C, for the hire of a car for n days, in two different garages, is shown in the boxes below.

Bill's Autos
$C = 11n + 60$

Carmart
$C = 20n$

    a If Fflur hires a car for 8 days, show that Bill's Autos is the cheaper of the two garages.

    b For how many days would Fflur have to hire the car for Carmart to be the cheaper garage?

DF
ES

8 $P = 1.5x + 2y$ is a formula to work out the total cost £P of x cups of tea and y cups of coffee.

    a Work out the cost of 3 cups of tea and 5 cups of coffee.

    b Peter buys 6 cups of tea and some cups of coffee. Work out the number of cups of coffee if the total cost is £15.

PB
ES

9 Here is a formula to change degrees centigrade, C, to degrees Fahrenheit, F.

$$F = \frac{9C}{5} + 32$$

    a On the 1st August, the temperature in New York was 79 °F.
On the 1st August, the temperature in Barcelona was 25 °C.
In which city was the temperature the greater?

    b Show that –20 °C is a higher temperature than –5 °F.

    c Work out the difference between 30 °C and 100 °F.

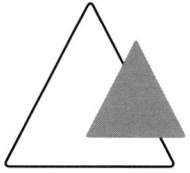

Algebra Strand 1 Starting Algebra Unit 5 Setting up and solving simple equations

PS PRACTISING SKILLS   **DF** DEVELOPING FLUENCY   **PB** PROBLEM SOLVING   **ES** EXAM-STYLE

PS **1** Solve the equations.

   a $a + 11 = 18$

   b $b - 3 = 9$

   c $5c = 65$

   d $7 = \dfrac{d}{4}$

PS **2** Solve the equations.

   a $3x - 2 = 13$

   b $5 - 4y = 17$

   c $2z + 15 = 7z + 9$

DF **3** Which of these equations does not have a solution $x = 3$?

   a $x + 5 = 8$

   b $7 - 2x = 1$

   c $\dfrac{10x}{6} = 5$

   d $1 - x = 4$

   e $2x - 5 = x - 2$

DF **ES** **4** Jen is x years old. Mary is twice as old as Jen. Rafa is 5 years older than Jen. The sum of their ages is 69 years.
How old will Rafa be in 10 years time?

PB **ES** **5** The lengths of the sides of a rectangle are given by $x + 1$, $3x - 2$, $9 - x$ and $x + 6$.
Work out the perimeter of the rectangle.

PB **ES** **6** Ewan pays £7.20 for 3 pies and 2 portions of chips.
Mel pays £4.50 for 5 portions of chips.
Sally buys 2 pies. How much does Sally pay?

PB **ES** **7** ABC is an isosceles triangle. Show that the greatest value for the perimeter of the triangle is 32.5.

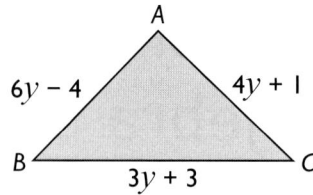

PB **ES** **8** Work out the size of the largest angle.

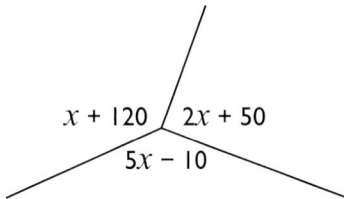

PB **ES** **9** Tom, Lucy and Sadiq share the driving on a journey of 145 miles. Tom drives x miles. Lucy drives three times as far as Tom. Sadiq drives 40 miles more than Lucy.

How many miles do they each drive?

PB **ES** **10** Ceri thinks of a number. She multiplies her number by 2 and then adds 3. Simon thinks of a number. He multiplies his number by 3 and then subtracts 2. Ceri and Simon both think of the same number.

What is the number they both thought of?

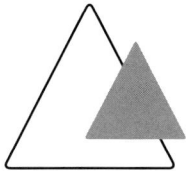

Algebra Strand 1 Starting Algebra Unit 6 Using brackets

PS — PRACTISING SKILLS   **DF** — DEVELOPING FLUENCY   **PB** — PROBLEM SOLVING   **ES** — EXAM-STYLE

PS **1** **a** Expand

   i $4(3m + 5)$

   ii $7(h - 3k)$.

   b Factorise

   i $12x - 8y$

   ii $6z + 6$.

PS **2** Orange juice costs £x per glass. Cola costs £y per glass.
ES Ham sandwiches cost £a each. Cheese sandwiches cost £b each.
Salad sandwiches cost £c each.

   a Sally, James and Hannah each have an orange juice and a
   cheese sandwich. Gethin and Sion each have a cola and a
   salad sandwich. Write down an algebraic expression for
   the total cost.

   b Three different people each choose a drink and a sandwich.
   The total cost is $3y + 2a + c$. Write down what each had.

DF **3** Write down an expression for
ES
   a the perimeter of this rectangle

   b the area of this rectangle.

   Give your answers in their simplest form.

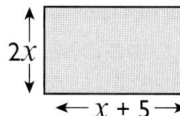

$2x$ ← $x + 5$ →

PS **4** **a** Expand

   i $3(b - 1) + 2(3 - b)$

   ii $5(a + 2) - 3(1 - a)$

   b Factorise

   i $6p^2 - 10p$

   ii $3c^2d + 9cd^2$.

5 Ella and Liam expand $2x(3x - 4)$.

This is what Ella wrote: $2x(3x - 4) = 6x^2 - 4$.

This is what Liam wrote: $2x(3x - 4) = 6x - 8x = -2x$.

  a Explain the mistake that each of Ella and Liam made.

  b Expand $2x(3x - 4)$.

6 CA, AB and BD are three sides of a quadrilateral of side $(x + 2)$ cm. The fourth side, X, is twice as long as the other three.

Show that the perimeter of the quadrilateral ABCD can be written $5x + 10$.

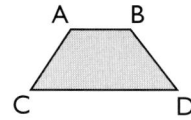

7 Colin is n years old. Della is 4 years older than Colin. Ezra is twice as old as Della.

Show that the sum of their ages is divisible by 4.

8 The cost of hiring a car is £C per day for the first 4 days. The cost is £$(C - 5)$ per day for all additional days. Steve hires a car for 10 days.

  a Write down an expression, in terms of C, for the total amount Steve has to pay. Give your answer in its simplest form.

Anne pays £$4(3C - 10)$ for the hire of a car.

  b How many days did Anne hire a car for?

9 The diagram shows a path around three sides of a lawn in a garden. The width of the path is x metres. The garden is in the shape of a rectangle of dimensions 20 m by 12 m.

Find, in terms of x, the perimeter of the lawn. Give your answer in its simplest form.

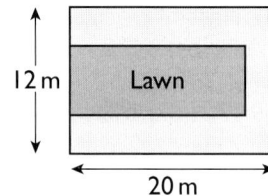

10 Glenda thinks of a whole number. She adds 4 to her number and then multiplies the result by 5. Isaac thinks of a whole number. He subtracts 3 from his number and then multiplies the result by 8.

Show that Glenda and Isaac could not possibly have thought of the same number.

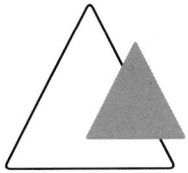

Algebra Strand 1 Starting Algebra Unit 7 Working with more complex equations

PS — PRACTISING SKILLS   DF — DEVELOPING FLUENCY   PB — PROBLEM SOLVING   ES — EXAM-STYLE

PB **1** Solve these equations.

   a $6t = 120$

   b $3x + 4 = 19$

   c $11 = 3 + \frac{1}{2}q$

PB **2** Solve these equations.

   a $5a + 2 = 3a + 14$

   b $6y - 3 = 3y + 30$

   c $7f - 4 = 3f - 16$

DF **3** Huw has been asked to solve $3.2g - 4.1 = 1.4g + 12.1$.

   a Explain why it is useful to multiply throughout by 10 before thinking about solving this equation.

   b Solve the equation for Huw. You must show your working.

DF **4** Solve each of these equations.

   a $1\frac{1}{2}h + \frac{3}{4} = \frac{1}{2}h + \frac{7}{8}$

   b $2\frac{1}{2}a - 5\frac{1}{2} = 2a + 7\frac{3}{4}$

PS **5** I think of a number, then double it and subtract 3. My answer is 19.

   a Write this information as an equation.

   b What number did I think of?

PS **6** The sum of n, $n + 3$ and $2n - 5$ is 30.

   a Write this information as an equation.

   b Solve your equation to find the value of n.

ES **7** I think of a number, x, then multiply by 6, finally I subtract 9. My answer is 51. Write an equation in terms of x and solve it.

ES **8** Two angles $4f°$ and $5f°$ make a straight line. Write an equation and solve it to find f.

Algebra Strand 1 Starting Algebra Unit 8 Solving equations with brackets

PS — PRACTISING SKILLS   DF — DEVELOPING FLUENCY   PB — PROBLEM SOLVING   ES — EXAM-STYLE

PB 1 Solve these equations.

    a $5(3x + 4) = 332$

    b $10(2g - 7) = 380$

PB 2 Solve these equations, show each stage of your working.

    a $5(2m - 3) = 3(2m + 4)$

    b $7(n - 8) = 2(2n + 9)$

DF 3 Yolanda thinks of a number. He adds 4 to his number and then multiplies the result by 5. His answer is 60.

    Write an equation and solve it to find the number he thought of.

DF 4 Expand these brackets and simplify.

    a $\frac{1}{2}(6m + 8)$

    b $\frac{3}{4}(8n + 16)$

PS 5 Anwen runs an animal rescue centre. She has x cats, $5x$ dogs and twice as many rabbits as cats. Anwen has 88 animals altogether.

    How many dogs does she have? Show your working by writing an equation and solving it.

PS 6 Simplify these.

    a $6 \times \frac{1}{3}(4x + 7)$

    b $\frac{1}{3} \times 9 (2x - 5)$

ES 7 Ben puts three angles together to form a straight line. The first angle is $2p°$, the second angle is $4p°$ and the third angle is $2(p + 3)°$.

    a Write an equation and solve it.

    b Write down the sizes of the three angles.

ES 8 Solve $3(5x + 6) = 4(2x + 7)$. Show all your working. Write your answer as a mixed number.

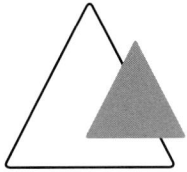

Algebra Strand 2 Sequences
Unit 3 Linear sequences

PS PRACTISING SKILLS   **DF** DEVELOPING FLUENCY   **PB** PROBLEM SOLVING   **ES** EXAM-STYLE

DF **ES** **1** Here are the first four terms of a sequence.

2   7   12   17

Here are the first four terms of another sequence.

4   7   10   13

The number 7 is in both sequences.

a Find the next two numbers that are in both sequences.

John says the number 202 is in both sequences.

b Is John right?

DF **ES** **2** Here are Pattern number 3 and Pattern number 4 of a sequence of patterns.

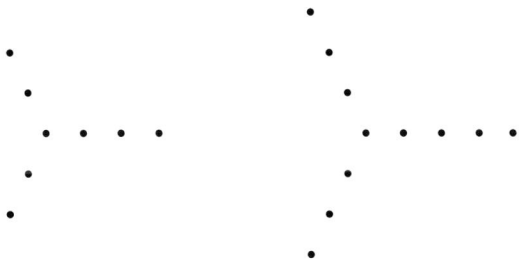

Pattern number 3   Pattern number 4

a Draw Pattern number 1 and Pattern number 2.

b Find the missing numbers in the table for this sequence of patterns.

Pattern number	1	2	3	4	5	10
Number of dots			8	11		

3 Here are the 2nd, 4th and 5th terms of a sequence.

___   15   ___   27   33

DF **a** Write down the 1st and 3rd terms of this sequence.

ES **b** Work out the product of the 6th and 7th terms of this sequence.

Ruth says that all the terms in this sequence are odd numbers.

PB **c** Show that Ruth is right.

PB **ES** **4** The anchor on a boat is lowered 3 metres with each turn of a handle. The anchor is already 5 metres below the surface of the sea.

    a How many metres below the surface of the sea will the anchor be after n turns of the handle?

The anchor hits the bottom of the sea after 64 turns of the handle.

    b How deep is the sea?

DF **ES** **5** Find the missing numbers in the table for this pattern of stars made with matchsticks.

Number of stars	1	2	3	4	8	20	n
Number of matches	10	19	28				

PB **ES** **6** A machine makes parts for a mobile phone. The list shows the number of parts that are made at 1 p.m. and at every 5 minutes after 1 p.m.

240   265   290   315   340

How many parts will be made at 2.30 p.m?

7 Here are the first four terms of a sequence.

150   138   126   114

PS   **a** Write down the next two terms in this sequence.

PB   **b** In what position is the first negative number in this sequence?

ES   **c** Show that the nth term of this sequence can be written in the form $6(a + bn)$.

PB **ES** **8** Here are the first five terms of a sequence.

3   7   11   15   19

    a **i** Write down the next two terms in this sequence.

       ii Explain how you got your answer to part **i**.

    b Find the 15th term of this sequence.

    c Write down, in terms of n, the nth term of this sequence.

PB **ES** **9** The nth term of sequence A is $2n + 1$. The nth term of sequence B is $4n - 3$.

    a How many of the first 10 numbers in sequence A are prime numbers?

    b Show that the sum of all corresponding numbers in each sequence is always an even number.

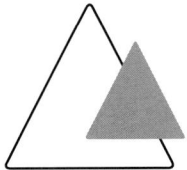

Algebra Strand 2 Sequences
Unit 4 Special sequences

PS — PRACTISING SKILLS   DF — DEVELOPING FLUENCY   PB — PROBLEM SOLVING   ES — EXAM-STYLE

DF **1** Here are the first eight terms of a sequence.

0   2   2   4   6   10   16   26

   a Describe the rule for working out the terms in this sequence.

   b Johan says: 'All the terms in this sequence must be even numbers.' Explain why Johan is right.

   c What is special about these numbers?

PS **ES** **2** Here are the first three patterns in a sequence of patterns.

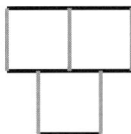

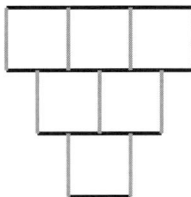

   a Write down the first 5 terms in the sequence formed by the vertical lines.

   b Show that the nth term of this sequence can be written as $\dfrac{n(n+3)}{2}$.

PS **ES** **3** The thickness of a piece of paper is 0.04 mm. Megan cuts the piece of paper in half. She places the pieces in a pile. Megan then cuts each piece of paper in the pile in half. She then places all the pieces in a pile. Megan continues to do this.

   a Work out the height of the pile after Megan has done this 5 times.

   b **i** Work out the height of the pile after Megan has done this 20 times.

      ii Explain why your answer to part i does not make sense.

DF **4** Here is a sequence made from equilateral triangles.

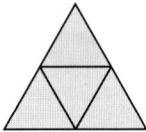

Pattern 1 is a 1 × 1 × 1 equilateral triangle

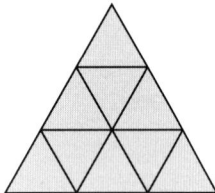

Pattern 2 is a 2 × 2 × 2 equilateral triangle

Pattern 3 is a 3 × 3 × 3 equilateral triangle

a Draw Pattern 4 and describe this equilateral triangle.

b i Write down the sequence of grey triangles.

  ii Describe this sequence.

c i How many triangles are in Pattern 4?

  ii Write down an expression, in terms of n, for the number of grey triangles in Pattern n.

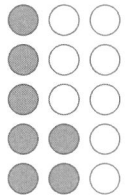

PB **ES** **5** Here is a sequence of patterns made with dots and straight lines.

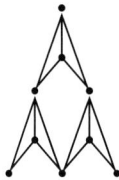

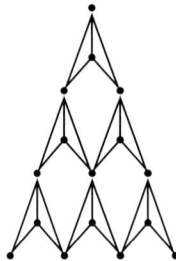

Pattern 1   Pattern 2   Pattern 3

a Find the missing numbers in the table.

Pattern number	1	2	3	4	10
Number of dots	4	9			
Number of lines	5	15			
Number of triangles	2	6			

b Write down, in terms of n, the nth term for the sequence of dots.

c i Show that the nth term for the sequence of triangles is $n^2 + n$.

  ii Use $n^2 + n$ to help you write, in terms of n, the nth term for the sequence of lines.

PB **ES** **6** Here are the first three terms of a sequence.

1   3   7

Alan says the next term in this sequence is 13. Becky says the next term in this sequence is 15.

a Explain how **both** Alan and Becky could be right.

b **i** Write down the 5th term of Alan's sequence.

ii Write down the 5th term of Becky's sequence.

PB **ES** **7** Here are the first four terms of a sequence.

16   8   4   2

a Write down the next three terms of this sequence.

b Which of the following expressions is the nth term of this sequence?

$$\dfrac{32}{2^{n+1}} \qquad \dfrac{n}{2} \qquad 2n \qquad \dfrac{32}{2^{n-1}} \qquad \dfrac{32}{2^{n}}$$

PB **ES** **8** P_n is the perimeter of an equilateral triangle. The next equilateral triangle is formed by joining the midpoints of the triangle. This is shown in the diagram.

$P_1 = 3s$

Write down P_2, P_3, P_4 and P_5 in terms of s.

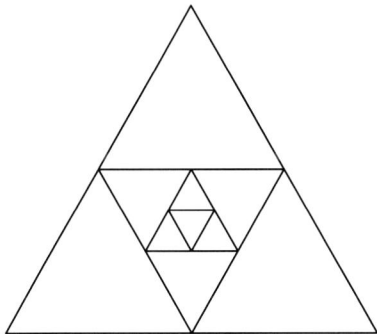

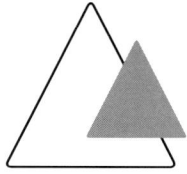

Algebra Strand 3 Functions and graphs Unit 1 Real-life graphs

PS PRACTISING SKILLS   **DF** DEVELOPING FLUENCY   **PB** PROBLEM SOLVING   **ES** EXAM-STYLE

PS **ES** **1** Electra is collecting information about the price of one litre of petrol in a 6-month period. Draw a line graph to show this information.

Month	Jan	Feb	Mar	Apr	May	Jun
Price in pence	112	115	117	115	116	118

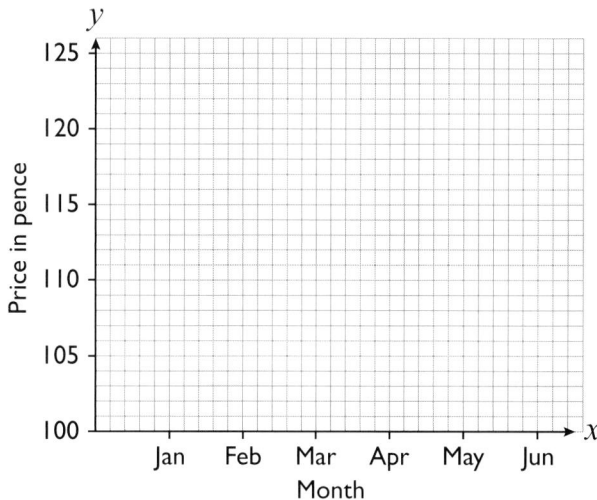

PS **ES**

2 You can use this graph to change between pounds and kilograms.

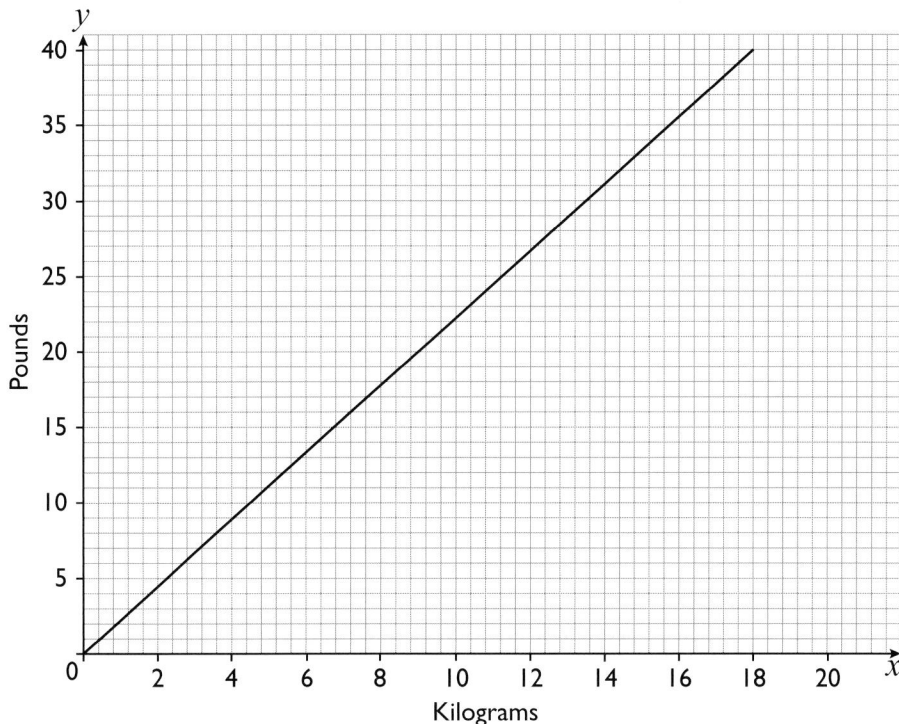

a Change 15 pounds to kilograms.

b Change 10 kilograms to pounds.

> 1 stone = 14 pounds

PB

c James weighs 12 stone 12 pounds. Iram weighs 80 kilograms.
Who is the heavier, James or Iram?

DF **3** Dafydd recorded the temperature at midday each day for a week. The diagram shows some information about his results.

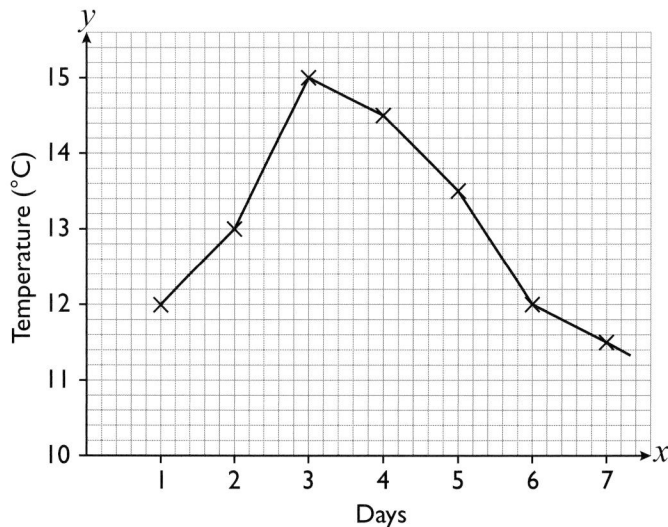

65

a Write down the range of the midday temperatures for this week.

b Between which two days was the change in temperature the greatest?

c Work out the average temperature for this week.

PB **ES** **4** Una travelled 20 km from home to a furniture shop. She then spent some time in the shop before returning home. This travel graph shows part of her journey.

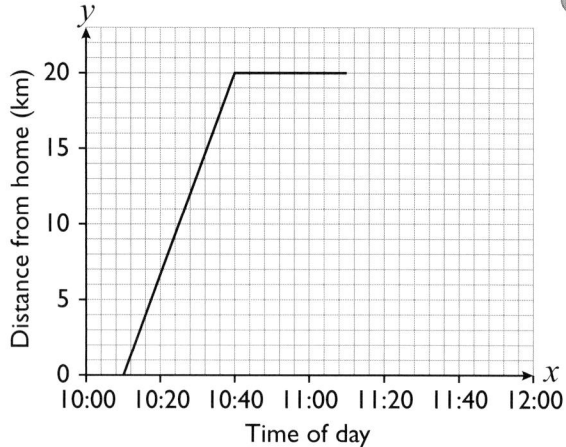

a Write down Una's distance from the furniture shop at 10:20.

Una left the shop at 11:10 to return home. On the way, at 11:30, she stopped for 10 minutes at a garage. The garage was 12 km from her home. Una arrived home at 12:00.

b i Work out Una's average speed from the garage to her home.

ii At which part of the whole journey did Una travel the quickest?

PB **ES** **5** This graph can be used to change between pounds (£) and US dollars ($).

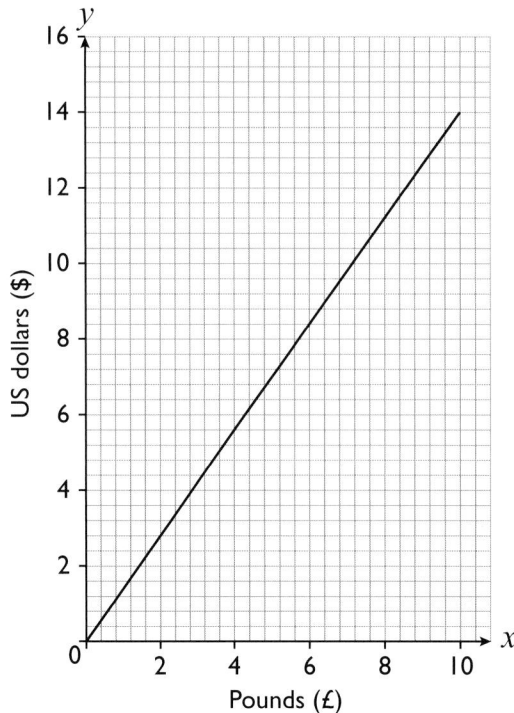

a Use the graph to change £5 to US dollars.

A laptop in the UK costs £460. The same model in the US costs $720.

b Where is the laptop the cheapest?

PB **ES** **6** This conversion graph can be used to change between litres and gallons. There are 8 pints in 1 gallon.

A dairy farm produces 720 pints of milk each day. The farmer sells the milk for 32p per litre.

How much money does the farmer sell his milk for each week?

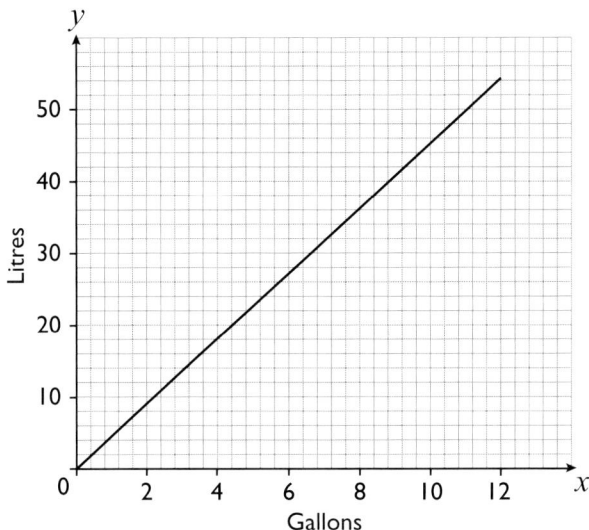

DF **ES** **7** Rosa travelled from her home to her friend's house 40 km away. She stayed for some time at her friend's house before returning home. Rosa left home at 10:10. She travelled at an average speed of 80 km/h. She stayed at her friend's house for half an hour. Rosa arrived home at 11:40.

Draw a travel graph to show Rosa's journey.

PB **8** Describe a situation that could be represented by this speed/time graph.

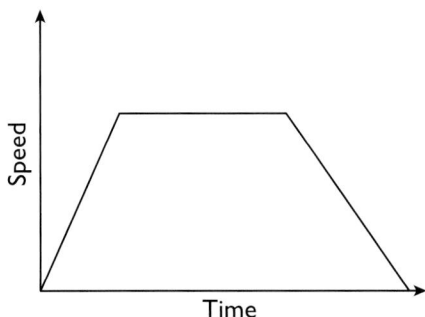

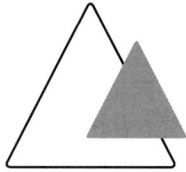

PS — PRACTISING SKILLS   DF — DEVELOPING FLUENCY   PB — PROBLEM SOLVING   ES — EXAM-STYLE

DF **1** Milk is sold at 90p per litre.

   a Work out the missing values in this table.

Number of litres	1	2	5	10	20	50	100
Cost in £	0.90			9			90

   b Draw a graph to show this information about the cost of milk.

   c Find the cost of 30 litres of milk.

   d How many litres of milk can be bought for £20?

DF **ES** **2** Lisa's company pays her travel expenses for each mile she travels.

   a Work out the missing values in this table.

Miles travelled	5	10	15	20	25	30	35	40
Expenses in £	4	8		16			28	

   b Draw a graph to show this information.

   c Lisa travels 28 miles. Work out how much her company pays her.

   d Lisa's company paid her £60 in travel expenses. How many miles did Lisa travel?

PB **ES** **3** This is a table of values for $y = \frac{1}{2}x + 5$.

x	-2	-1	0	1	2	3	4
y		4.5	5				7

   a Complete the table of values.

   b Using 2 mm graph paper, draw the graph of $y = \frac{1}{2}x + 5$.

   Use values of x-axis -2 to 4, and values of y-axis -1 to 8.

PB **ES** **4** This rule can be used to work out the time, in seconds, it takes to download music tracks.

> Time = 25 × number of music tracks + 10

a Work out the missing information in this table of values.

Number of tracks	2	4	6		10	12
Time in seconds	60			210		

b Draw a graph to show the time it takes to download music tracks.

c How many tracks can be downloaded in 10 minutes?

PB **ES** **5** Vijay lives 3 kilometres from his school. The travel graph shows Vijay's journey to school one day.

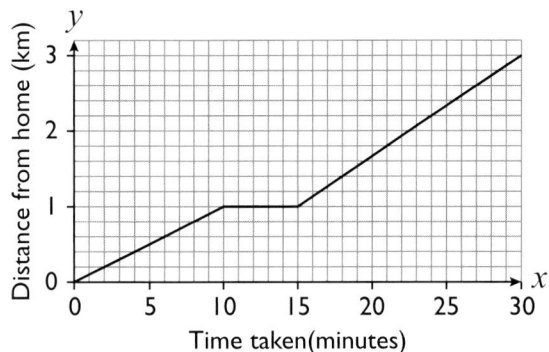

a Describe the three stages in Vijay's journey to school.

On another day, Vijay left home at 08:15. At 08:32 he stopped at a shop to buy a drink. The shop is 1.4 km from school.
At 08:38 he left the shop and carried on walking to school.
He arrived at school at 08:45.

b Draw a travel graph to show this journey.

PB **ES** **6** This is a table of values for $y = 3x + 4$.

x	−2	−1	0	1	2	3
y		1				13

a Work out the missing values for this table.

b Use your table to draw the graph of $y = 3x + 4$ from $x = -2$ to $x = 3$.

c Find the value of x when $y = 8$.

PB **ES**

7 Steffan goes on holiday to Prague. The currency in Prague is the Czech Crown (czk). The exchange rate is £1 = 30czk.

a Draw a graph that could be used to convert between £ (pounds) and czk (Czech Crown).

Steffan bought a suitcase in Prague. He paid 750czk for the suitcase. In London the same model of suitcase costs £34.

b How much money did Steffan save by buying the suitcase in Prague?

PB **ES**

8 Here is a rule to work out the cost, in pounds, of printing invitations at Printshop.

Cost (£C) = number of invitations (n) × 1.25 + 4

a Write down a formula for C in terms of n.

b Draw a graph of C against n.

At Print-4-U, the cost is £20 for printing 12 of each invitation. Martin wants 24 invitations printed.

c Which shop should Martin buy his invitations from?

PB **ES**

9 Pat delivers parcels. The table shows the cost of delivering parcels for different journeys.

Distance in miles	10	20	30	40	50
Cost in £	20	30	40	50	60

a Draw a graph to show this information.

For each parcel Pat delivers there is a fixed charge plus a charge for each mile.

b Use your graph to work out the fixed charge and the charge for each mile.

Vanessa also delivers parcels. For each parcel Vanessa delivers it costs £1.50 for each mile. There is no fixed charge.

c Compare the cost of having a parcel delivered by Pat with the cost of having a parcel delivered by Vanessa.

DF **ES**

10 Draw the graph of $y = 2x + 3$ for values of x from $x = -3$ to $x = 1$.

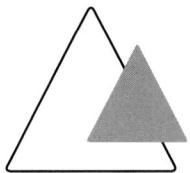

Geometry and Measures Strand 1 Units and scales Unit 7 Converting approximately between metric and imperial units

PS ─ PRACTISING SKILLS   **DF** ─ DEVELOPING FLUENCY   **PB** ─ PROBLEM SOLVING   **ES** ─ EXAM-STYLE

PB **1** Convert these volumes to litres.

    a 4 gallons

    b 9 gallons

    c 15 gallons

PB **2** Convert these distances.

    a 5 inches to cm

    b 20 miles to km

    c 1200 km to miles

DF **3** Heddwen is 163 cm tall. Linda is 5 foot 6 inches tall.
Who is taller? By how much? Give your answer in centimetres.

DF **4** A fairground ride says, 'Minimum height 4 foot 10 inches.'
ES Jac is 142 cm tall. Can he go on the ride? Give a reason for
your answer and show your working.

PS **5** On Monday, Tomos uses 8 gallons of fuel, costing £1.15 per litre.
How much does the fuel Tomos used on Monday cost?

PS **6** A section of a recipe says, '5 oz flour, 8 oz sugar.' Convert these to
suitable metric units.

ES **7** Lois sees a road sign, 'speed limit 30 miles per hour', which means
30 miles in one hour. How many kilometres in one hour would this be?

ES **8** A rectangle measures $2\frac{1}{2}$ inches by $1\frac{1}{4}$ inches. What are these
measurements in centimetres?

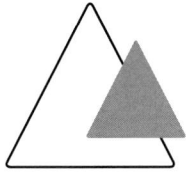

Geometry and Measures
Strand 1 Units and scales
Unit 8 Bearings

PS PRACTISING SKILLS   **DF** DEVELOPING FLUENCY   **PB** PROBLEM SOLVING   **ES** EXAM-STYLE

PS **1** Answer these

     a Measure the bearing of Oxford from Bath

     b Measure the bearing of Bath from Oxford.

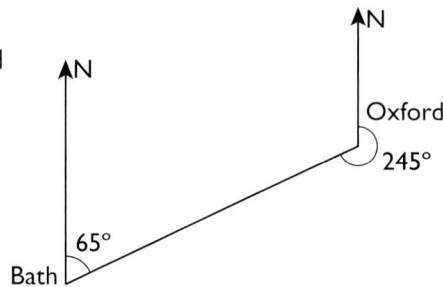

PS **2** **a** Write down the bearing of these compass directions.

       i West

       ii South-East

     b Write down the compass points with these bearings.

       i 090°

       ii 225°

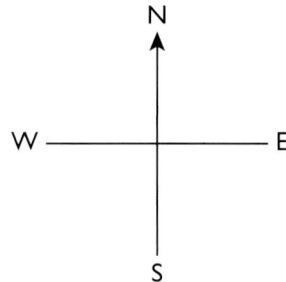

DF **ES** **3** The diagram shows two coastguard stations, P and Q. The bearing of Q from P is 080°. There is a boat at point B. The bearing of B from P is 140°. The bearing of B from Q is 240°. Find the angle PBQ.

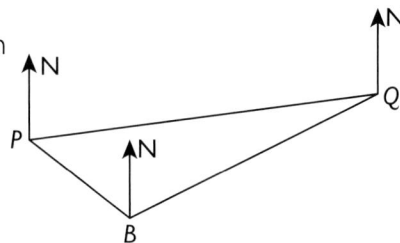

PB **ES** **4** An aeroplane flew 60 km from A to B, then 80 km from B to C, and then back from C to A. The bearing of B from A is 120°. The bearing of C from B is 270°.

     a Using a scale of 1 cm to represent 10 km, draw an accurate diagram to show the aeroplane's journey.

     b **i** What bearing must the aeroplane travel on to get from C to A?

       ii What is the distance from C to A?

DF **5** Ipswich is on a bearing of 080° from Sudbury.

ES **a** What is the bearing of Sudbury from Ipswich?

Ipswich is also North-East of Colchester.

b Find the bearing of Ipswich from Colchester.

c Work out the back bearing of Colchester from Ipswich.

DF **6** The diagram shows a ship, S, and its position from two lighthouses, P and Q.

Find the bearing of

a P from Q

b S from P

c Q from P

d P from S.

Q is South-West of S.

e Find the bearing of S from Q.

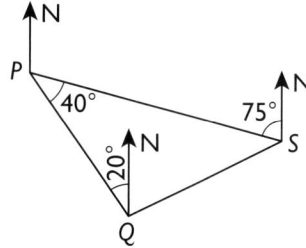

PB **7** Tegid sails his boat from Cromer on a bearing of 060° for 6 km.

ES He then changed direction and sailed on a bearing of 150° for 8 km.

a Draw an accurate diagram to show Tegid's boat trip. Use a scale of 1 cm to represent 1 km.

Tegid then travels back to Cromer along a straight line.

b What bearing does Tegid travel on to get back to Cromer?

c How far does he travel in total?

PB **8** Four buoys A, B, C and D are arranged so that

ES B is on a bearing of 60° from A
C is on a bearing of 105° from A
C is on a bearing of 150° from B
A is on a bearing of 330° from D.
Explain why ABCD is a square.

PB **9** A plane is travelling due South at 200 miles an hour. At 10 a.m.

ES the bearing of an island from the plane is 120°. At 10.30 a.m.
the bearing of the island from the plane is 060°. The plane will
not pass within 75 miles of the island. Explain why.

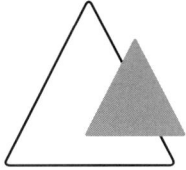

Geometry and Measures
Strand 1 Units and scales
Unit 9 Scale drawing

PS — PRACTISING SKILLS   DF — DEVELOPING FLUENCY   PB — PROBLEM SOLVING   ES — EXAM-STYLE

PS ES 1 A map has a scale of 1:25 000. The distance between the church and the garage in a village is 2 cm on the map.

a Work out the actual distance between the church and the garage.

The actual distance between two petrol stations is 4 km.

b How far apart are the petrol stations on the map?

DF 2 Rosie follows these instructions when she takes part in an orienteering competition.

> Start at the town clock and walk North for 200 metres.
> Walk East for 150 metres and then South for 100 metres.

a Use a scale of 1 cm represents 20 m to draw a scale drawing of Rosie's walk.

b How far is Rosie from her starting point?

DF ES 3 Megan wants to find the length of the sloping roof of the end of her shed. She cannot reach the top of the shed so draws a scale drawing of the end of the shed.

Find the length of the slope.

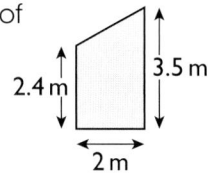

2.4 m   3.5 m

2 m

DF 4 Here is an accurate plan of a garden drawn on a scale of 1 cm represents 4 m.

Copy and complete the table to show the actual measurements of the garden.

Measurement	Drawing	Actual
Length of lawn		
Width of lawn		
Radius of pond		
Width of veg plot		
Length of patio		
Width of patio		

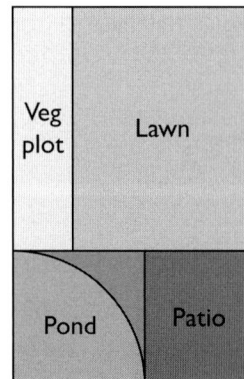

Veg plot   Lawn

Pond   Patio

74

DF **ES** **5** Tyson wants to draw a scale drawing of the town gardens.
He is going to use a sheet of paper that is 70 cm long by 44 cm wide.
The town gardens are rectangular in shape and have a length of
280 m and a width of 150 m.

Explain what scale Tyson should use to make his scale drawing
as large as possible.

PB **ES** **6** Here is a 3-D sketch of the extension Ellie wants to
add to her house. The overall height of the
extension must be 4.3 m.

Using a scale drawing, find the height of
the wall.

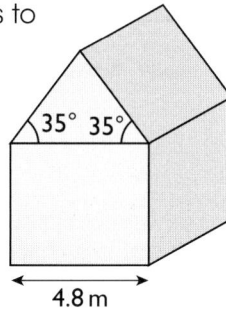

35° 35°

4.8 m

PB **7** The gym in Sophie's school will be set
out with desks for an exam for
150 students. The gym is 30 m long and
15 m wide. The desks are 60 cm wide.
There must be 1.2 m between each desk.

The first desk is put in the bottom left
hand corner of the gym alongside
the walls. The diagram shows the
position of 4 of the desks.

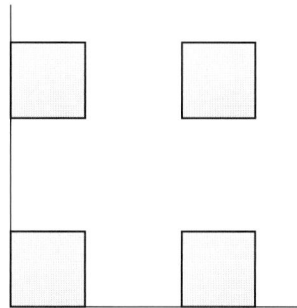

Show, by drawing, that the gym is big
enough to hold enough desks for the exam.

PB **ES** **8** Dafydd finds an old plastic model of an aeroplane in his loft. The scale
of the model is 1:72. The length of the model is 15 cm.

Find the length of the aeroplane in feet and inches.
Use 1 inch = 2.54 cm and 12 inches = 1 foot.

PB **ES** **9** Ben sails his boat from port, P, on a bearing of 120° for 25 km.
He then sails on a bearing of 240° for 30 km.

What is the bearing and distance the boat would have to travel
in order to get back to port P?

Geometry and Measures
Strand 1 Units and scales
Unit 10 Compound units

PS — **PRACTISING SKILLS**   DF — DEVELOPING FLUENCY   PB — **PROBLEM SOLVING**   ES — **EXAM-STYLE**

PS **1** Work these out.

  a Natalie drove at an average speed of 44 mph for two and a half hours. Work out how far she travelled.

  b Jason drove 330 km in 6 hours. Work out his average speed.

  c Bavna walked from her home to school at an average speed of 4.5 km/h. The school was 1.5 km from her home. Work out how long it took her.

PS **ES** **2** Mike ran 100 m in 9.8 seconds.

  a Work out his average speed in m/s.

  b Change your answer to km/h.

PS **ES** **3** Gareth's car uses 5 litres of petrol when it travels 30 miles. Susan's car uses 8 litres of petrol when it travels 50 miles.

  Whose car has the higher average rate of petrol consumption?

DF **ES** **4** Becca is going to grow a new lawn from seed. Her lawn is a rectangle 17 m long and 5 m wide. She buys a 2 kg box of grass seed which is enough to grow a 100 m² lawn.

  How many grams of grass seed will she have left?

DF **ES** **5** Toni's train leaves Bath railway station at 09:15. It arrives in London at 10:30. It travels 120 miles from Bath to London.

  Work out its average speed in mph.

DF **ES** **6** The speed of light is 186 000 miles per second. The Sun is 93 million miles from the Earth.

  Work out how long it takes a ray of light to travel from the Sun to the Earth. Give your answer in minutes and seconds.

PB **ES** **7** The speed limit on motorways in France is 130 km/h. The speed limit on motorways in the UK is 70 mph.

  Find the difference in the two speed limits. Use the fact that 5 miles = 8 km.

76

PB
ES

8 Sophie has a fish pond in the shape of a cuboid. She needs to empty the full pond to clean it out.

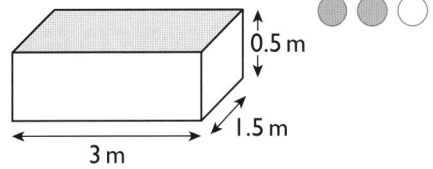

She puts all the fish into another pond and pumps the water out at a rate of 25 litres per minute. She starts pumping out the water at 10 a.m.
At what time will the pond be empty?
Use the fact that $1 m^3 = 1000$ litres.

PB
ES

9 Mia is going to visit her mother who lives 230 miles away. She drives at an average speed of 60 mph for an hour and a half. She then stops for a 15 minute rest. She travels the remaining part of the journey at an average speed of 70 mph.

Work out Mia's overall average speed for the whole journey.

PB **10** Tomos uses this conversion graph to change between litres and gallons.

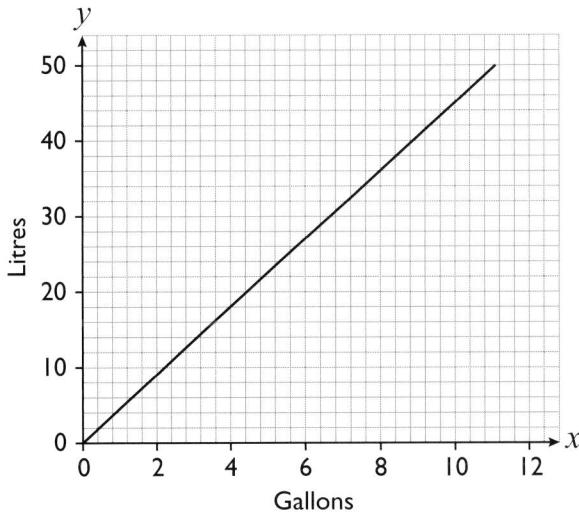

a i Change 5 gallons to litres.
ii Change 45 litres to gallons.

Tomos uses on average 0.5 litres of heating oil per hour to run his heating system. The heating system works for 14.5 hours a day for 200 days of the year. Tomos has two empty tanks in which he stores the heating oil. Tank P holds 1000 litres of oil. Tank Q holds 300 gallons of oil.

Tomos buys enough heating oil to last a whole year. He completely fills Tank P and puts the rest of the oil into Tank Q.

b How many gallons does Tomos put into tank Q?

Tomos decides to completely fill up tank Q as he gets a special deal on heating oil. The extra oil costs 32p per litre.

c How much does it cost to completely fill Tank Q?

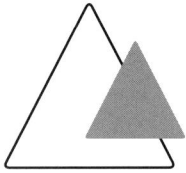

Geometry and Measures Strand 2 Properties of shapes Unit 5 Angles in triangles and quadrilaterals

PS — PRACTISING SKILLS   DF — DEVELOPING FLUENCY   PB — PROBLEM SOLVING   ES — EXAM-STYLE

PB 1 Find the size of angle a.

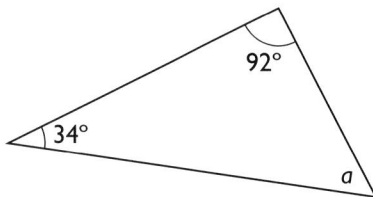

PB 2 Find the size of angle b.

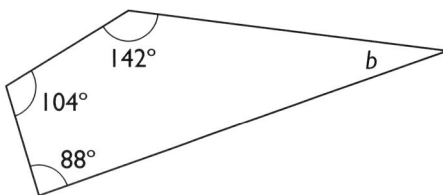

DF PS 3 Find the size of angles c and d.

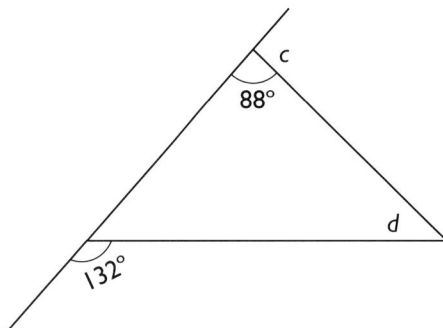

DF
PS
4 Find the size of angle e.

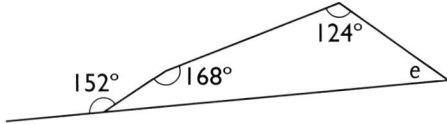

ES **5** Find the size of angle a.

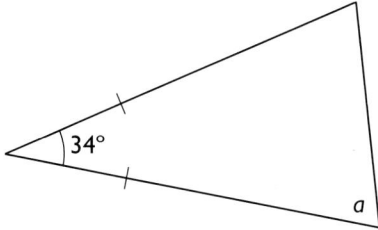

ES **6** Find the size of angle a.

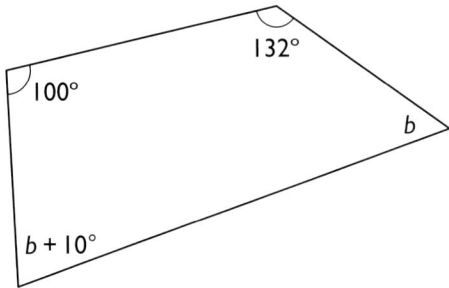

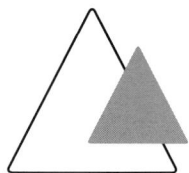

Geometry and Measures
Strand 2 Properties of shapes
Unit 6 Types of quadrilateral

PS — PRACTISING SKILLS   **DF** — DEVELOPING FLUENCY   **PB** — PROBLEM SOLVING   **ES** — EXAM-STYLE

PS **1** Name the quadrilaterals that have   ●○○

    a two pairs of opposite sides equal and parallel

    b four equal sides

    c diagonals that cross at 90°.

PS **2** **a** Draw a trapezium that has one acute angle only.   ●○○

    b Draw a kite that has one right angle only.   ●○○

    c Draw an arrowhead that has one right angle only.   ●○○

    d Explain why it is not possible to draw a trapezium with only one   ●○○
    right angle.

DF **3** Draw an *xy* co-ordinate grid with *x*- and *y*-axes from 0 to 8.   ●○○

    a Plot the points P at (2, 8) and Q at (6, 5).

      i Draw a rectangle with PQ as a diagonal.

    b Plot the point, R, at (7, 1).

      i Find the co-ordinates of S to make PQRS a parallelogram.

DF **4** Draw an *xy* co-ordinate grid with *x*-and *y*-axes from –2 to 8.   ●○○

    a Plot the points A at (7, 2) and C at (1, 6).

      i Draw a rhombus with AC as a diagonal.

    b Plot the point B at (5, 6).

      i Find the co-ordinates of a possible position of D to make
      ABCD an isosceles trapezium.

DF **5** PQRS is a parallelogram.   ●○○
    Find the missing angles P, Q and R of
    the parallelogram. Explain your answer.

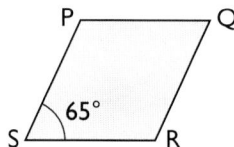

PB **ES** **6** ABCD is an isosceles trapezium. BEC is an isosceles triangle.

AD = BC = CE

Find the size of angle D. Give reasons for your answer.

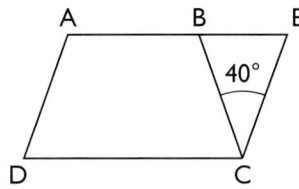

PB **ES** **7** EFGH is a rhombus. JHG is a straight line.

Explain why angle EGF is 64°.

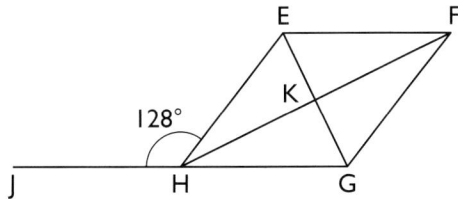

PB **ES** **8** ABCD is a rhombus.

P is the midpoint of AB.
Q is the midpoint of BC.
R is the midpoint of CD.
S is the midpoint of DA.
Explain why PQRS is a rectangle.

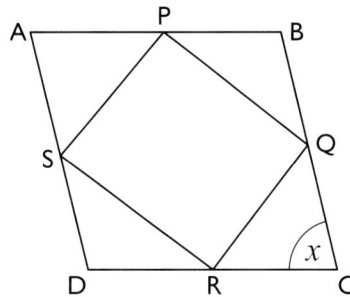

PB **ES** **9** PQST is a parallelogram. QRS is an isosceles triangle.

Work out the size of angle SQR. Give reasons for your answer.

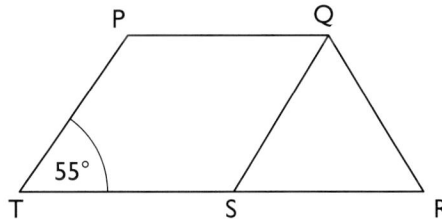

PB **ES** **10** ABCE is a parallelogram. ADE is a right-angled triangle.

Work out the size of angle EAD.
Give reasons for your answer.

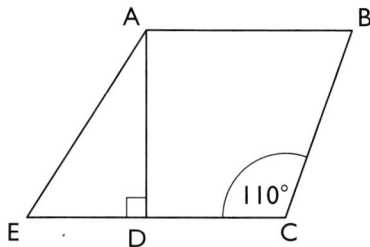

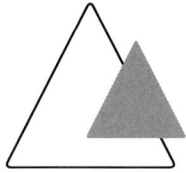

Geometry and Measures
Strand 2 Properties of shapes
Unit 7 Angles and parallel lines

PS PRACTISING SKILLS **DF** DEVELOPING FLUENCY **PB** PROBLEM SOLVING **ES** EXAM-STYLE

PS **1** Write down the name of the marked angles.

a

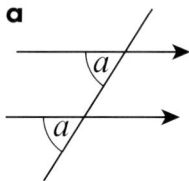

b

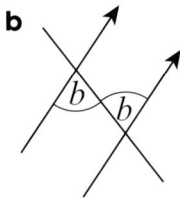

c

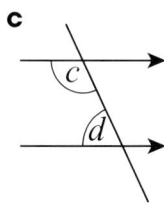

PS **2** Find the missing angles in these diagrams.
Give reasons for your answer.

a

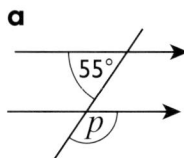

b

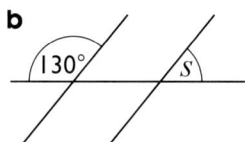

PS **3** Find the missing angles in these diagrams.

a

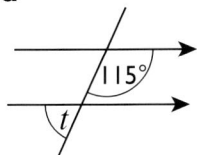

b

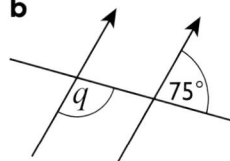

PS **4** Explain fully why the two allied (co-interior) angles marked on this diagram are supplementary.

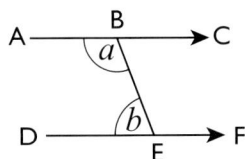

DF **5** Here is a diagram of a gate.
Find the missing angles. Give reasons for your answer.

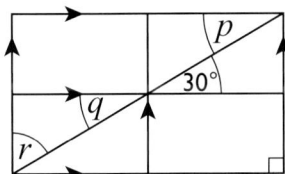

DF **6** PQRS is a rectangle. SRT is a straight line. PQTR is a parallelogram.
ES Find the value of angle RPS.

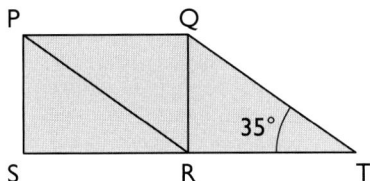

DF **7** ABDE is a parallelogram. BCD is an isosceles triangle.
ES Find the size of angle AED. Give reasons for your answer.

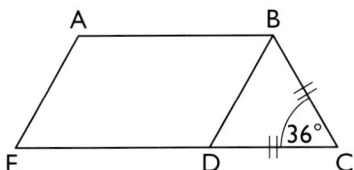

PB
ES
8 The diagram is made up from a rectangle and a parallelogram.
Find the size of the angle marked *a*.

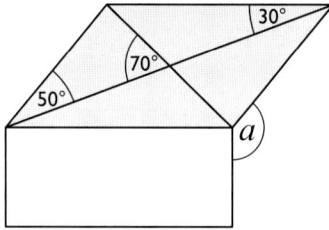

PB
ES
9 EFG is an isosceles triangle. Explain why.

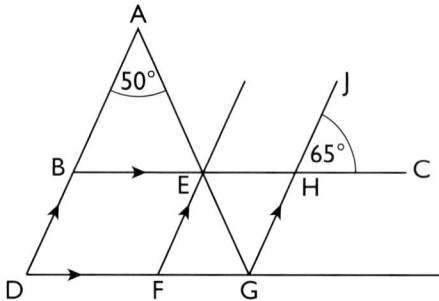

PB
ES
10 a Use this diagram to explain why the three angles of a triangle add up to 180°. You must give reasons with your explanation.

b Write down a fact in your explanation.

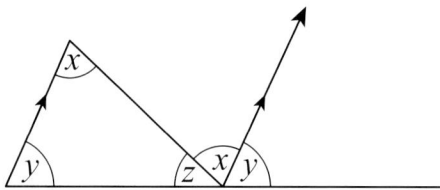

PB
ES
11 Explain why AB and CD are parallel lines. Give reasons for each step of your explanation.

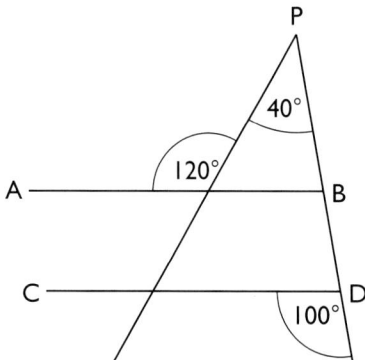

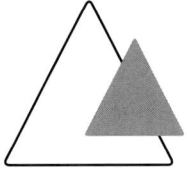

Geometry and Measures
Strand 2 Properties of shapes
Unit 8 Angles in a polygon

PS – **PRACTISING SKILLS** **DF** – **DEVELOPING FLUENCY** **PB** – **PROBLEM SOLVING** **ES** – **EXAM-STYLE**

PS **1** Work out the size of the exterior angle and the interior angle
of these regular shapes.

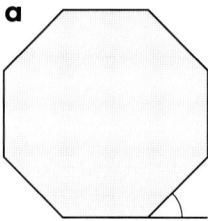

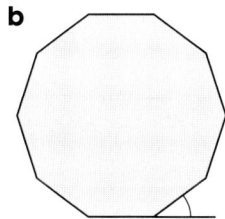

a

b

PS **2** Find the number of sides in a regular polygon that has an

    a exterior angle of 20°

    b interior angle of 108°.

DF **ES** **3** The interior angle of a regular polygon is 140°. Find the number of
sides in the polygon.

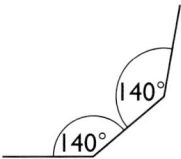

PB **ES** **4** Find the size of angle *x*.

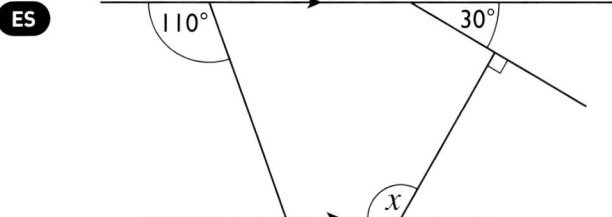

PB **ES** **5** The diagram shows a regular octagon and a regular hexagon. Find the size of the angle marked *m*.

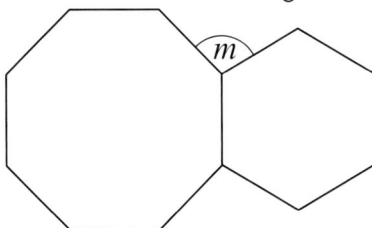

PB **ES** **6** Here is a regular dodecagon, centre O. Explain why OPQ makes an equilateral triangle.

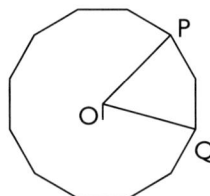

PS **ES** **7** Here is a regular octagon. Two of its diagonals are drawn on the shape. Find the size of angle *p*.

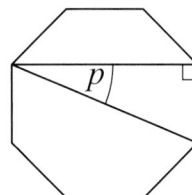

DF **ES** **8** The sum of the interior angles of a polygon is 2340°. Work out the number of sides in the polygon.

DF **ES** **9** Three regular polygons meet at a point. One of the polygons has an interior angle of 60°. Another polygon has an interior angle of 144°.

Find the number of sides in each of the three polygons.

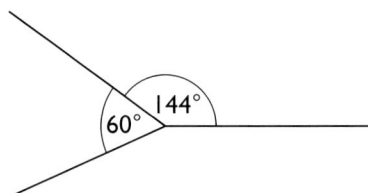

PB **ES** **10** The diagram shows a regular heptagon and a regular pentagon drawn on the same base. Work out the size of the angle marked *t*.

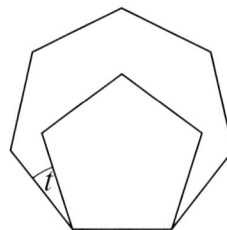

PB **ES** **11** Explain, giving reasons, why it is possible to tile a floor using regular dodecagons and equilateral triangles that have the same length side. You should state any assumptions that you make.

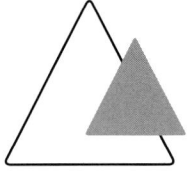

Geometry and Measures
Strand 3 Measuring shapes
Unit 2 Finding area and perimeter

PS ▸ PRACTISING SKILLS   DF ▸ DEVELOPING FLUENCY   PB ▸ PROBLEM SOLVING   ES ▸ EXAM-STYLE

PB **1** Find the area and perimeter of the rectangle. State the unit in your answer. ●○○

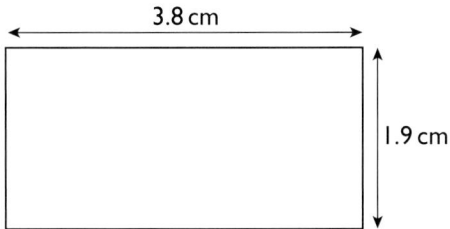

3.8 cm

1.9 cm

PB **2** Find the area of the triangle. State the unit in your answer. ●○○

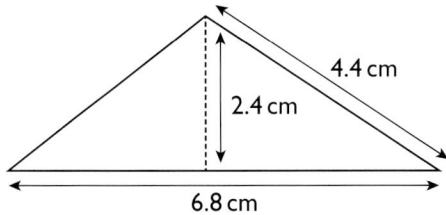

4.4 cm

2.4 cm

6.8 cm

DF **3** Find the area of the parallelogram. State the unit in your answer. ●●○

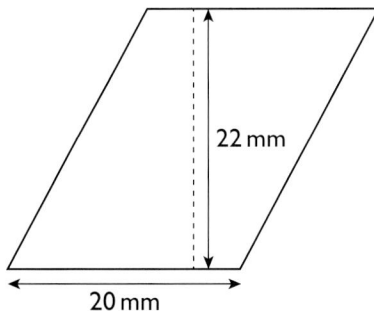

22 mm

20 mm

DF **4** Find the area of the trapezium. State the unit in your answer. ● ● ●

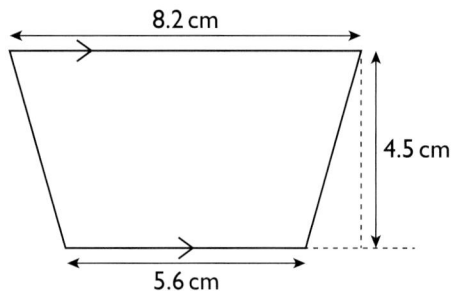

8.2 cm

4.5 cm

5.6 cm

PS **5** Find the perimeter of the trapezium. State the unit in your answer. ● ● ●

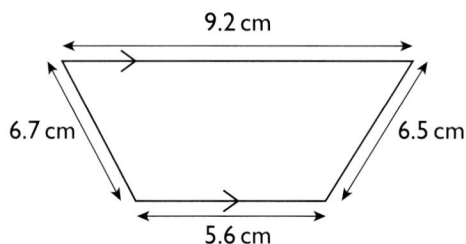

9.2 cm

6.7 cm

6.5 cm

5.6 cm

PS **6** Find the perimeter of the composite shape shown. State the unit in your answer. ● ● ●

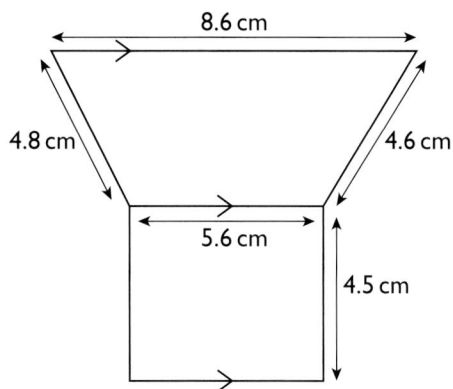

8.6 cm

4.8 cm

4.6 cm

5.6 cm

4.5 cm

ES **7** Answer these. State the units in your answers.

    a Find the perimeter of the complete rectangle shown.

    b Find the area of the complete rectangle shown.

    c Find the area of triangle ABC. Show your calculation.

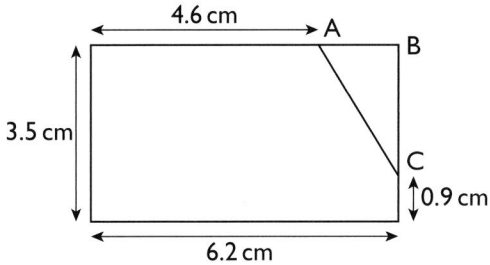

ES **8** Rhodri's driveway is a composite shape made from joining a trapezium, a square and a parallelogram. Rhodri wants to treat his driveway with biodegradable weed killer. Each bottle of weed killer will treat $8\,m^2$ and costs £1.20.

    a How much will it cost Rhodri to treat his drive? Remember he needs to buy complete bottles of weed killer.

    b Will Rhodri have more or less than half a bottle of weed killer left over? You must show your working.

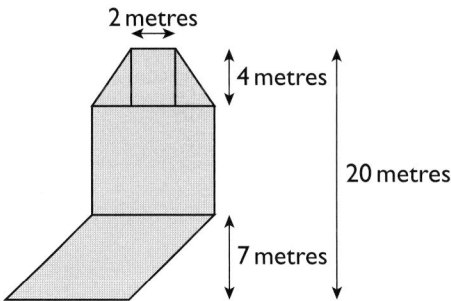

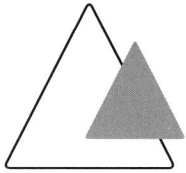

Geometry and Measures
Strand 3 Measuring shapes
Unit 3 Circumference

PS PRACTISING SKILLS   **DF** DEVELOPING FLUENCY   **PB** PROBLEM SOLVING   **ES** EXAM-STYLE

PS **1** Find the circumference of these circles with radius

a 4 cm

b 7.5 m

c 0.5 km.

Write your answers correct to two decimal places.

Don't forget
$C = \pi D$
or
$C = 2\pi r$

PS **2** Find the circumference of these circles with diameter

a 6 cm

b 3.5 m

c 0.25 km.

Write your answers correct to one decimal place.

PS **3** **a** A circle has a circumference of 78.5 cm. Find the diameter of the circle. Give your answer correct to 1 decimal place.

b A circle has a circumference of 1 m. Find the radius of the circle. Give your answer correct to 2 decimal places.

DF **ES** **4** Derek makes a semi-circular flower bed. The radius of the flower bed is 90 cm. Find the perimeter of the flower bed.

DF **ES** **5** Carlie makes a cake with a diameter of 25 cm. She puts a ribbon around the middle of the cake. Carlie allows an overlap of 2 cm for the ribbon.

How long is the ribbon? Give your answer to the nearest centimetre.

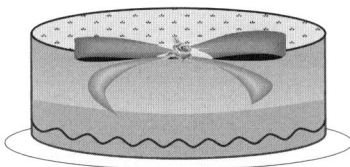

PB **ES** **6** Jamie makes jewellery. She makes a brooch from a semicircle and an equilateral triangle. Find the perimeter of the brooch. Give your answer correct to 2 decimal places.

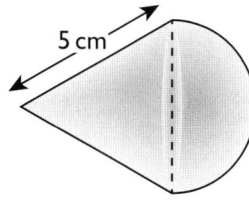

5 cm

PB **ES** **7** Naga is making a fish pond in her garden. The fish pond is in the shape of a quarter circle. The radius of the circle is 1.5 metres. Naga is planning to create a path around the pond.

Find the perimeter of the pond. Give your answer to the nearest cm.

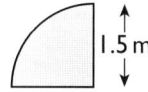

1.5 m

PB **ES** **8** Wyn is marking out a netball court in the school hall. The court is made up from three rectangles and two semicircles. Wyn is using tape to mark out the lines. Each roll of tape contains 50 m of tape.

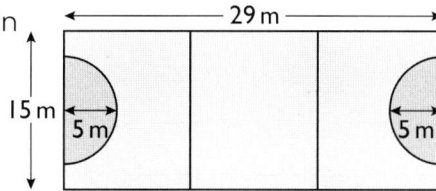

29 m

15 m

5 m

5 m

Here is a diagram that shows the lines on the court. Work out how many rolls of tape Wyn needs to buy.

PB **ES** **9** Hefin is making a stained glass window. He uses pieces of lead to hold the glass in place. The rectangular window is made from two semicircles and 6 straight edges.

Work out the total length of the lead to make the window. Give your answer to the nearest centimetre.

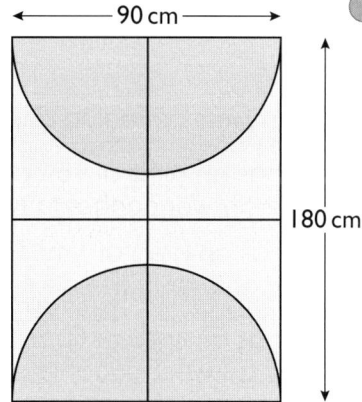

90 cm

180 cm

PB **ES** **10** Rose is making a flower bed. The flower bed is made from two semicircles. The radius of the large semicircle is 3 m. The radius of the small semicircle is 1 m.

Rose is going to put lengths of edging strip along each edge of the flower bed. The edging strip is sold in lengths of 1.8 m.

How many edging strips will Rose need to buy?

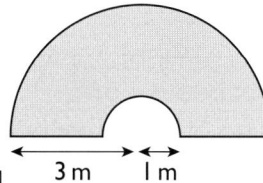

3 m   1 m

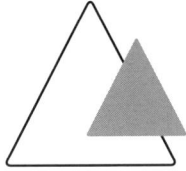

Geometry and Measures
Strand 3 Measuring shapes
Unit 4 Area of circles

PS — PRACTISING SKILLS   DF — DEVELOPING FLUENCY   PB — PROBLEM SOLVING   ES — EXAM-STYLE

PS **1** Find the area of these circles with radius

    a 5 cm

    b 7 m

    c 3.2 cm.

    Give your answers correct to one decimal place.

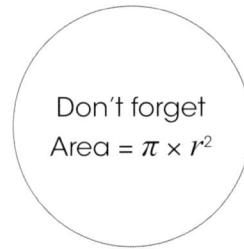

> Don't forget
> Area = $\pi \times r^2$

PS **2** Find the area of these circles with diameter

    a 6 cm

    b 5 m

    c 0.8 km.

    Give your answers correct to one decimal place.

PS **3** **a** A circle has an area of 15.7 cm^2. Find the radius of the circle.
    Give your answer correct to two decimal places.

    b A circle has an area of 1 m^2. Find the diameter of the circle.
    Give your answer to the nearest centimetre.

DF **4** **a** A circle has an area of 50 cm^2. Find the circumference of the circle.
    Give your answer correct to one decimal place.

    b A circle has a circumference of 314 cm. Find the area of the circle.
    Give your answer correct to the nearest metre^2.

DF **ES** **5** Mo makes a semicircular flower bed. The radius of the flower bed is 1.5 m.

Find the area of the flower bed. Give your answer correct to 2 decimal places.

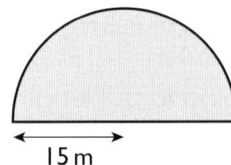

15 m

PB **ES** **6** Mia makes a semicircular carpet. The area of the carpet is 2.55 m^2.
Find the perimeter of the rug. Give your answer to the nearest cm.

PB
ES
7 Naga feeds the fish in her fishpond. The fishpond is in the shape of a quarter circle. For every square metre of the area of the pond she gives the fish 25 g of fish food each day.

How many grams of fish food does she need to give the fish? Give your answer to the nearest gram.

2.5 m

PB
ES
8 The diagram shows a circular pond surrounded by a path. The pond has a radius of 2.5 m. The path is 1 metre wide. The path is going to be covered with wood bark. Wood bark is sold in bags that cost £2.99 each. Each bag contains enough bark to cover 0.75 m².

Work out the cost of the wood bark needed to cover the path.

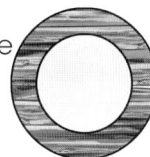

PB
ES
9 Ifan is making a lawn. The lawn is in the shape of half a ring made from two semicircles. The semicircles have the same centre. The radius of the large semicircle is 15 m. The radius of the small semicircle is 5 m.

Ifan buys 1 kg boxes of lawn seed at £9 per box. Each kg of lawn seed covers 25 m².

How much does it cost Ifan to buy the grass seed?

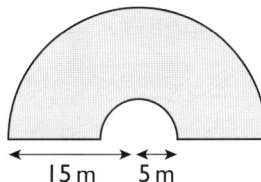

15 m   5 m

DF
ES
10 Paul makes a brooch. He makes it from a semicircle and two quarter circles of metal. The diameter of the semicircle is 4.5 cm. The radius of the large quarter circle is 2.5 cm. The radius of the small quarter circle is 1.5 cm.

Find the area of the brooch.

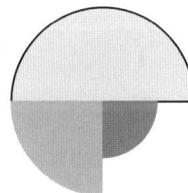

PB
ES
11 This shape is made from a right-angled triangle, two semicircles and a quarter circle.

Find the area of this shape.

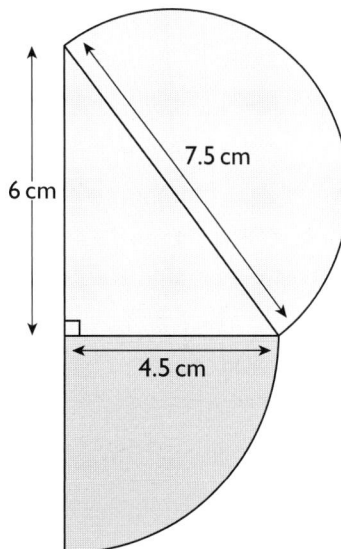

7.5 cm

6 cm

4.5 cm

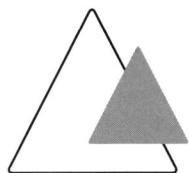

Geometry and Measures Strand 4 Construction Unit 2 Constructions with a ruler and protractor

PS PRACTISING SKILLS   DF DEVELOPING FLUENCY   PB PROBLEM SOLVING   ES EXAM-STYLE

PB 1 Use a ruler and protractor to accurately draw the triangle shown. Measure the length f.

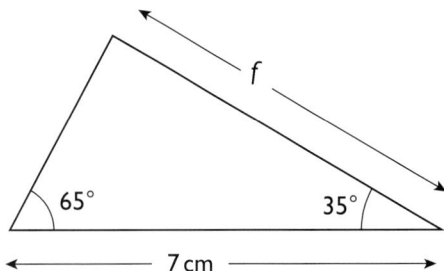

65°   35°
7 cm

PB 2 Use a ruler and protractor to accurately draw the triangle shown. Measure the length g.

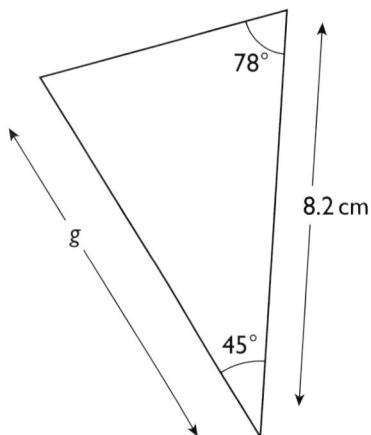

78°
8.2 cm
g
45°

DF 3 Use a ruler and protractor to accurately draw the triangle shown.
Measure the length r.

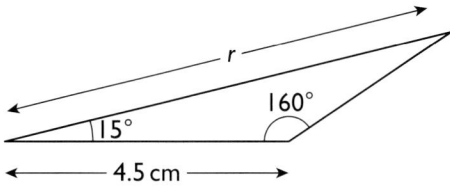

DF 4 Use a ruler and protractor to accurately draw the triangle shown.
Measure the length s.

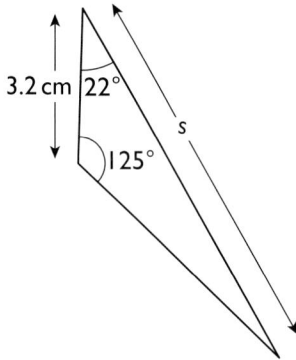

PS 5 Construct a rhombus with each side of length 7 cm. The angles should be 55°, 125°, 55° and 125°.

PS 6 Construct a parallelogram with sides of length 6.5 cm and 8.2 cm. The angles should be 45°, 135°, 45° and 135°.

ES 7 Accurately draw the parallelogram ABCD.
Write down the lengths of each of the diagonals, AC and DB.

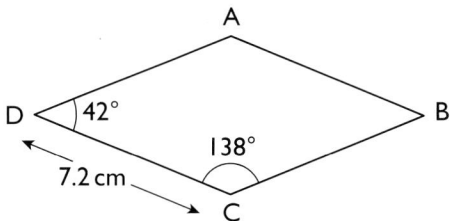

ES **8** The diagram shows two right-angled triangles.
Draw the diagram accurately to find the length m.

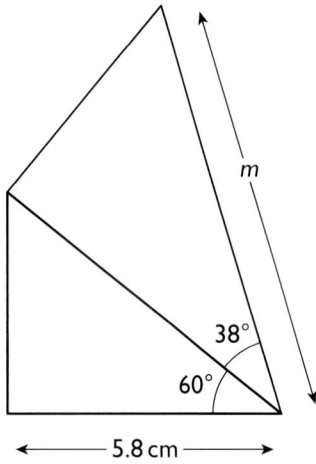

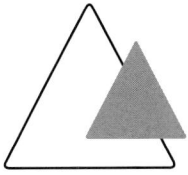

Geometry and Measures Strand 4 Construction Unit 3 Constructions with a pair of compasses

PS PRACTISING SKILLS   **DF** DEVELOPING FLUENCY   **PB** PROBLEM SOLVING   **ES** EXAM-STYLE

PB **1** Use a pair of compasses to construct a triangle with length of sides 5 cm, 6 cm and 8 cm.

PB **2** Use a pair of compasses to construct a triangle with length of sides 6.2 cm, 7.1 cm and 9.4 cm.

DF **3** Start by drawing a line of length 8 cm.

    a Construct an angle of 60°.

    b Bisect your angle of 60°.

DF **4** Start by drawing a line of length 10 cm.

Construct, using a pair of compasses, the perpendicular bisector of your 10 cm line.

PS **5** Start by drawing a line of 10 cm, which must not be horizontal.

Mark a point somewhere below your line, at least 4 cm away from your line.

Now construct, using a pair of compasses, a perpendicular line from your point to your line.

PS **6** Construct, using a pair of compasses and a ruler, a rhombus with sides of length 8 cm. The angles should be 60°, 120°, 60° and 120°.

ES **7** Draw a line of length 12 cm.

    a Construct, using a pair of compasses, the perpendicular bisector of your line.

    b Using a pair of compasses, bisect one of the 90° angles formed.

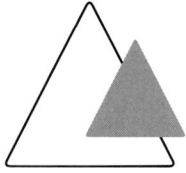

Geometry and Measures
Strand 5 Transformations
Unit 3 Translation

PS **1** Copy the diagram and answer the questions.
DF   **a** Translate the triangle $\begin{pmatrix} 2 \\ -3 \end{pmatrix}$.
PB   **b** Write down the co-ordinates of each of the vertices of your translated triangle.
ES

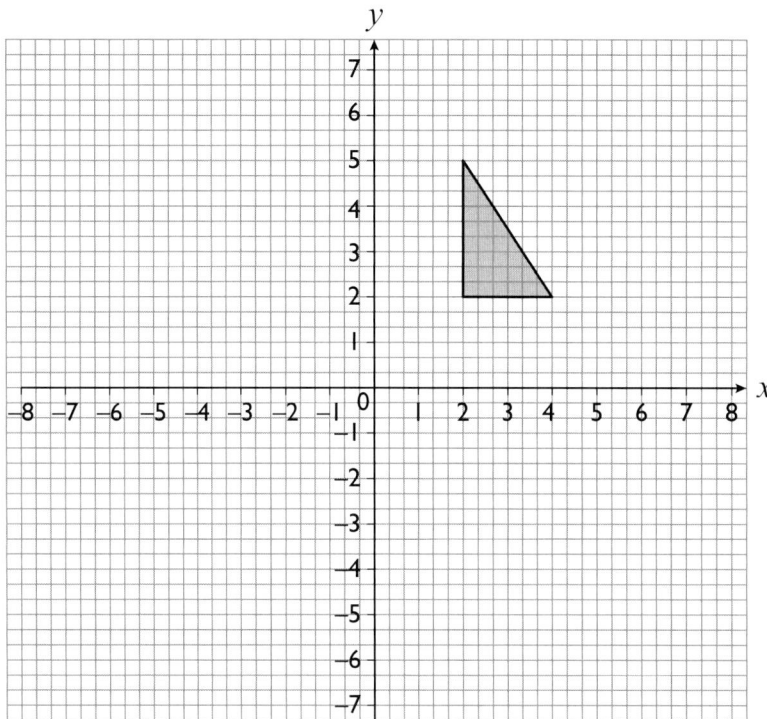

PS **2** Copy the diagram and answer the questions.
DF   **a** Translate the triangle $\begin{pmatrix} -4 \\ 3 \end{pmatrix}$.
PB   **b** Write down the co-ordinates of each of the vertices of your translated triangle.
ES

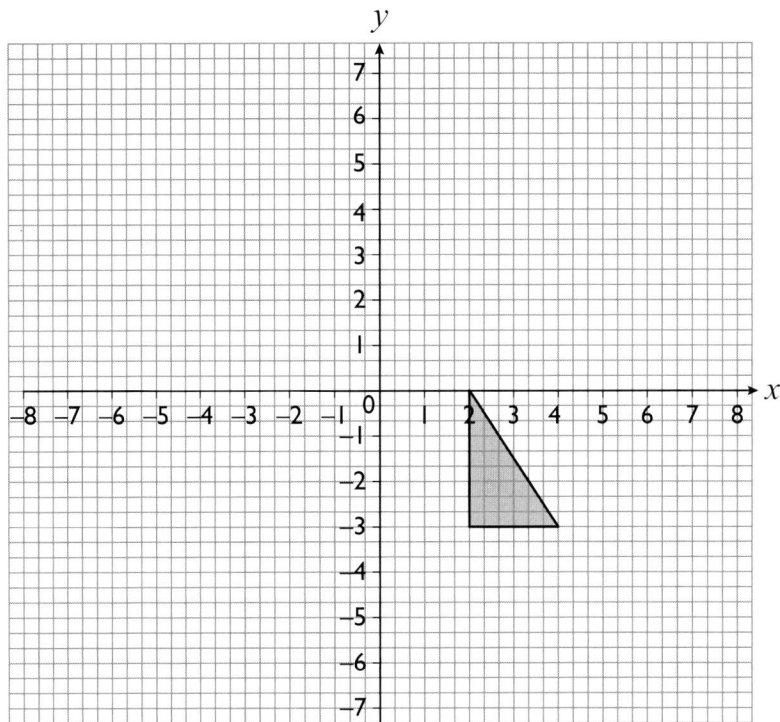

PS
DF
PB
ES

3 Copy the diagram and answer the questions.

   a Translate the triangle $\begin{pmatrix} -1 \\ -3 \end{pmatrix}$.

   b Write down the co-ordinates of each of the vertices of your translated triangle.

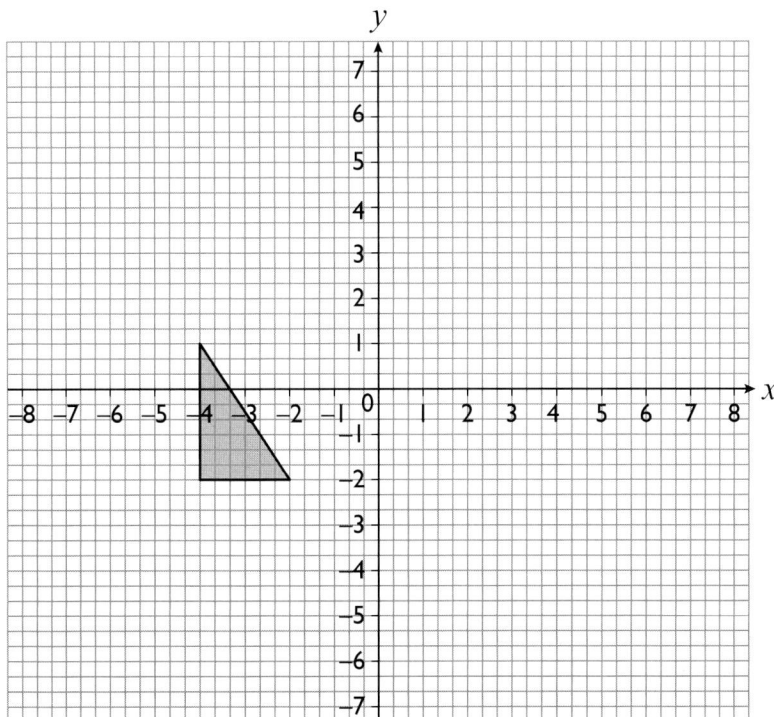

99

PS
DF
PB
ES

4 Copy the diagram and answer the questions.

    a Translate the triangle $\begin{pmatrix} 2 \\ 8 \end{pmatrix}$.

    b Write down the co-ordinates of each of the vertices of your translated triangle.

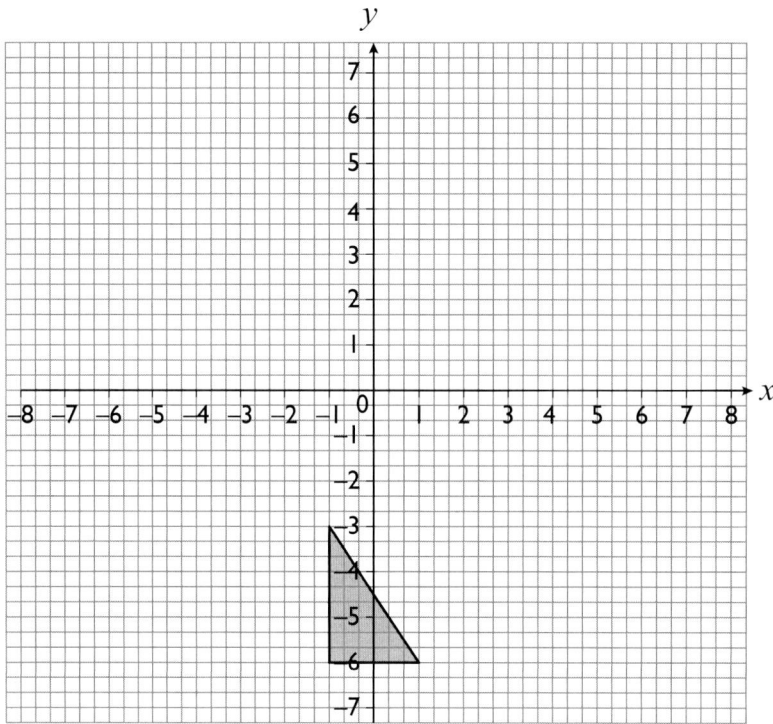

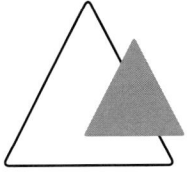

Geometry and Measures
Strand 5 Transformations
Unit 4 Reflection

PS PRACTISING SKILLS   **DF** DEVELOPING FLUENCY   **PB** PROBLEM SOLVING   **ES** EXAM-STYLE

DF
PB
1 Copy the diagram and answer the questions.

    a Reflect the triangle shown in the x-axis.

    b Write down the co-ordinates of each of the vertices of your reflected triangle.

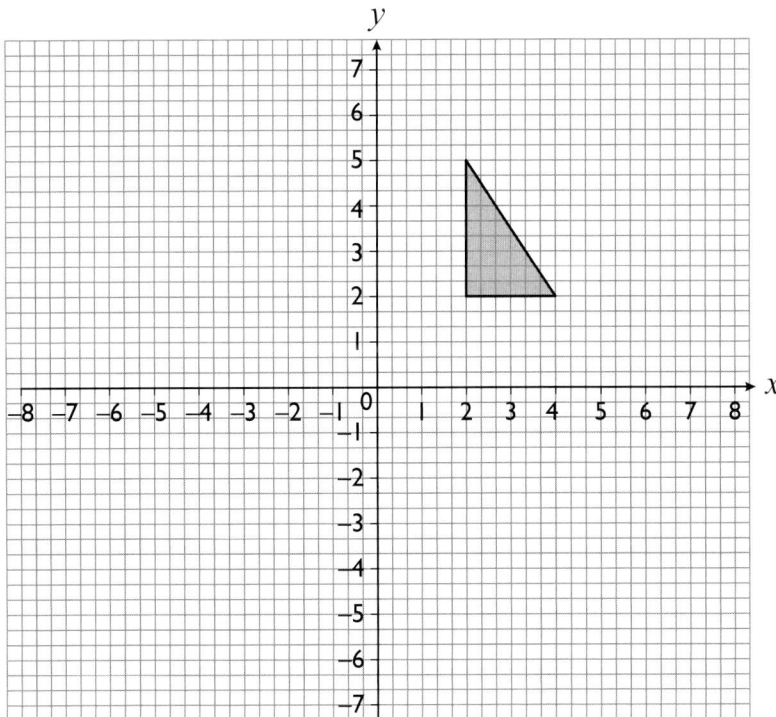

DF
PB

2 Copy the diagram and answer the questions. ●●○

a Reflect the triangle shown in the y-axis.

b Write down the co-ordinates of each of the vertices of your reflected triangle.

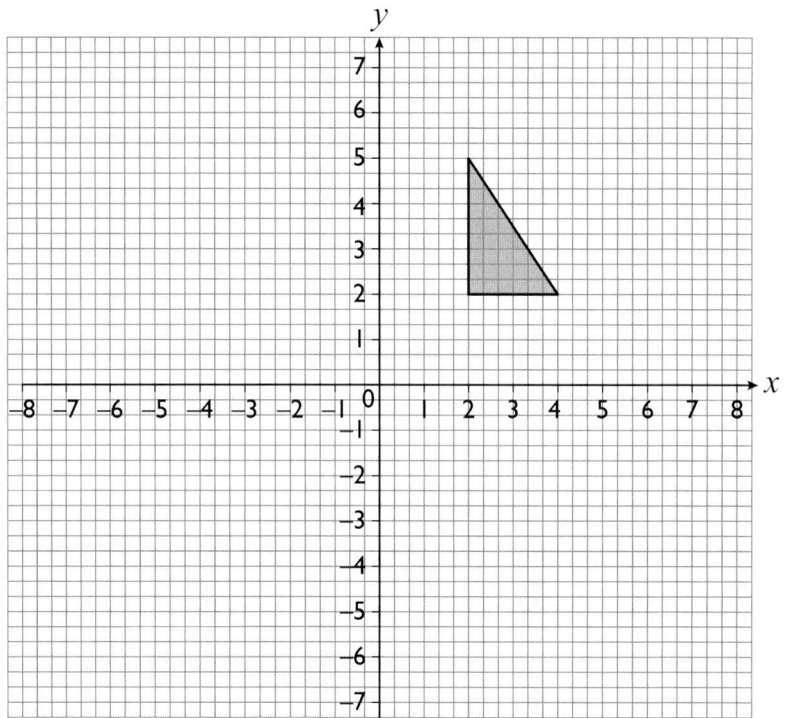

PS
ES

3 Copy the diagram and answer the questions. ●●●

a Reflect the triangle shown in the line $x = -1$.

b Write down the co-ordinates of each of the vertices of your reflected triangle.

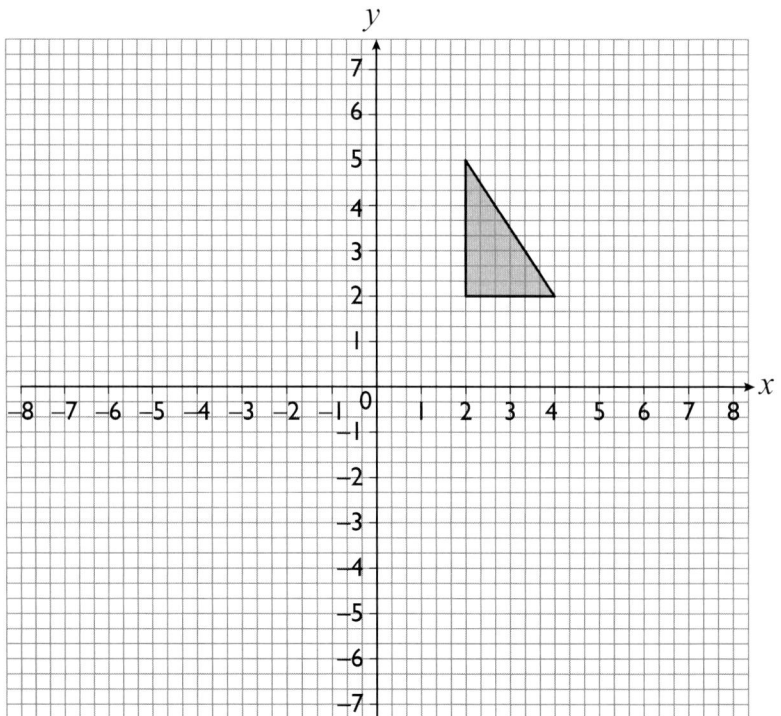

PS

ES

4 Copy the diagram and answer the questions.

a Reflect the triangle shown in the line $y = 1$.

b Write down the co-ordinates of each of the vertices of your reflected triangle.

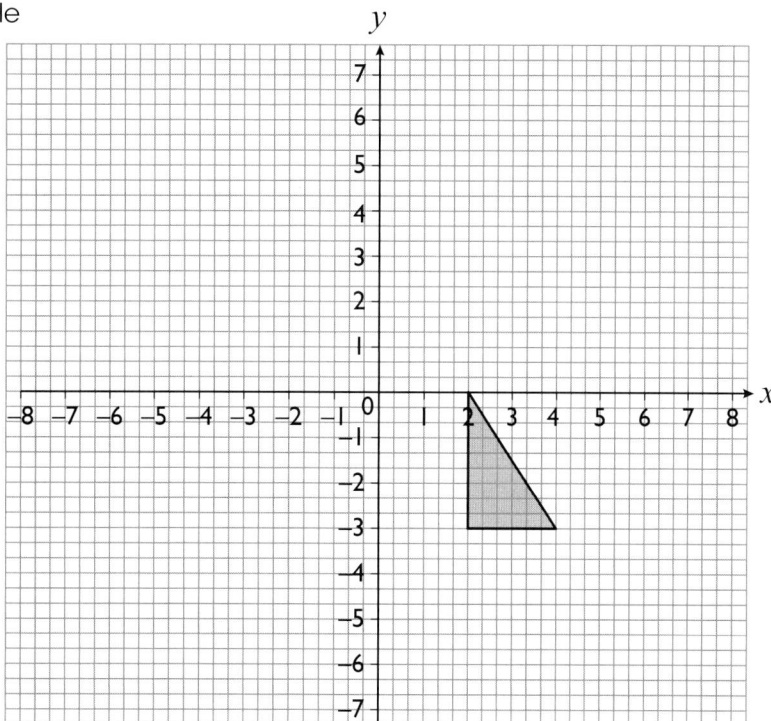

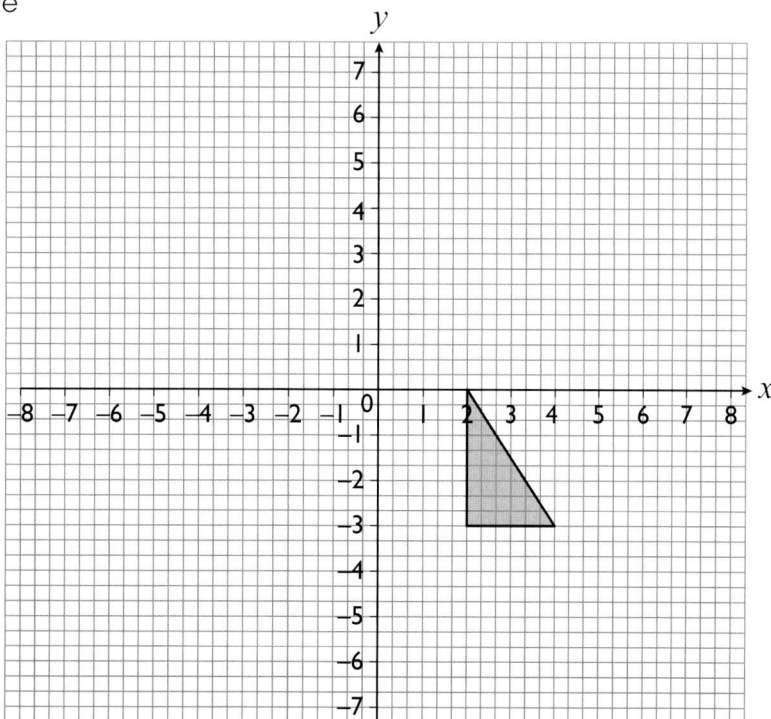

PS

ES

5 Copy the diagram and answer the questions.

a Reflect the triangle shown in the line $y = x$.

b Write down the co-ordinates of each of the vertices of your reflected triangle.

PS

ES

6 Copy the diagram and answer the questions.

a Reflect the triangle shown in the $y = -x$.

b Write down the co-ordinates of each of the vertices of your reflected triangle.

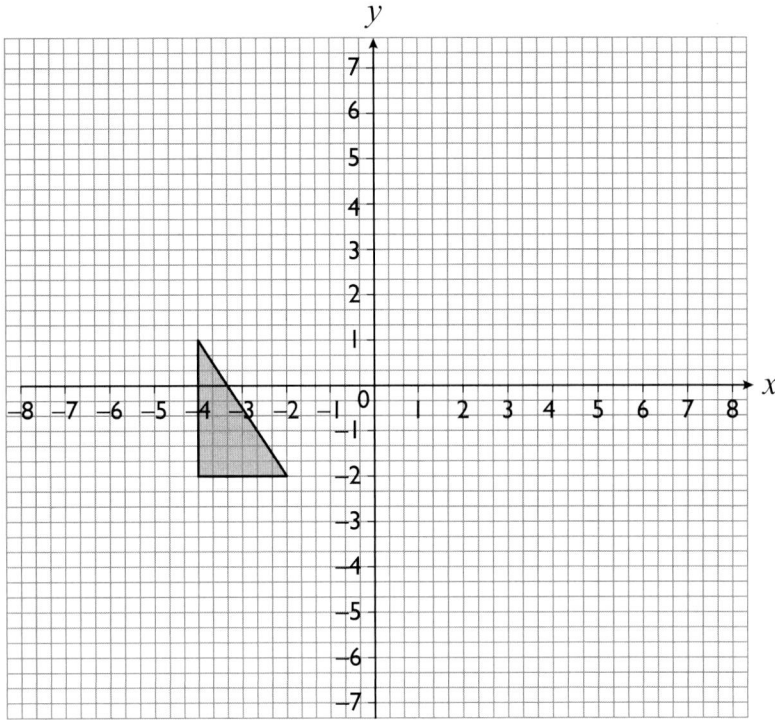

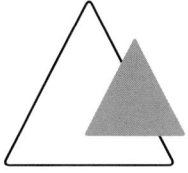

Geometry and Measures
Strand 5 Transformations
Unit 5 Rotation

PS — PRACTISING SKILLS   DF — DEVELOPING FLUENCY   PB — PROBLEM SOLVING   ES — EXAM-STYLE

DF
PB
1 Copy the diagram and answer the questions.

   a Rotate the triangle shown 180° about the origin (0, 0).

   b Write down the co-ordinates of each of the vertices of your rotated triangle.

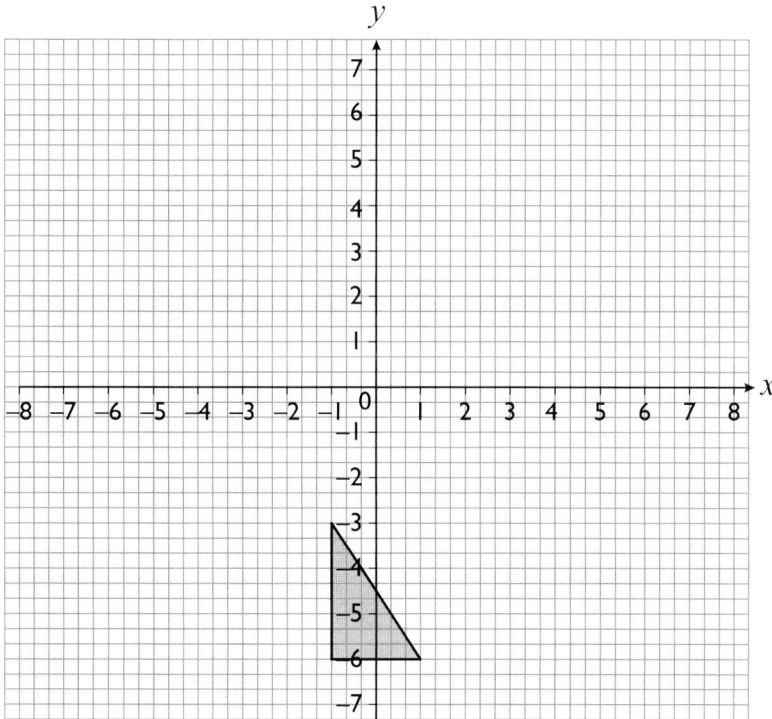

DF **2** Copy the diagram and answer the questions.

PB

a Rotate the triangle shown 90° clockwise about the origin (0, 0).

b Write down the co-ordinates of each of the vertices of your rotated triangle.

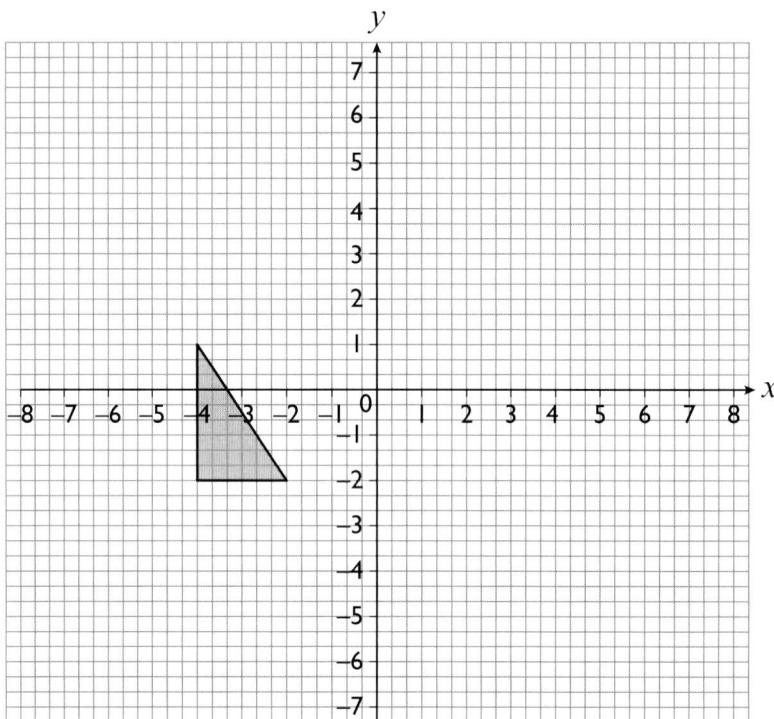

DF **3** Copy the diagram and answer the questions.

PB

a Rotate the triangle shown 90° anticlockwise about the origin (0, 0).

b Write down the co-ordinates of each of the vertices of your rotated triangle.

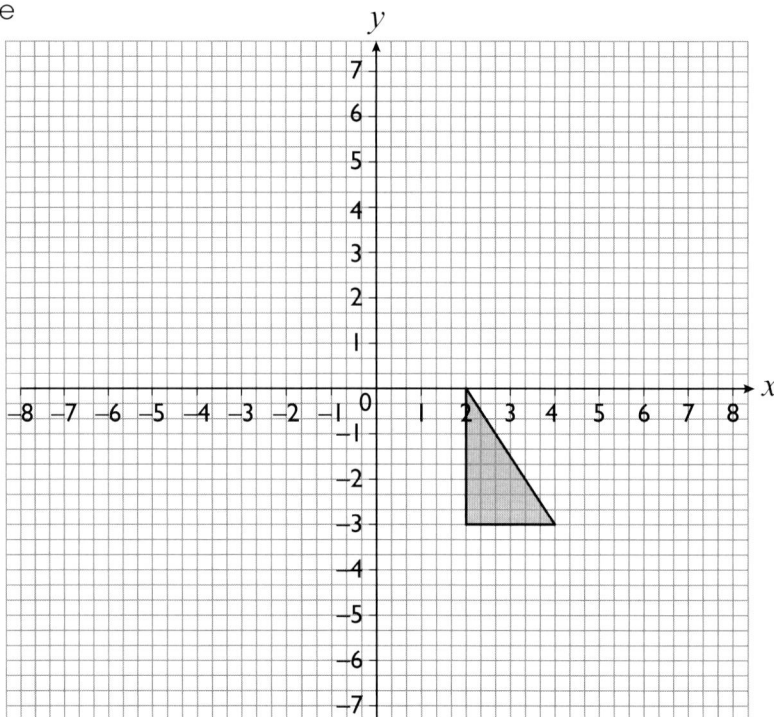

PS 4 Copy the diagram and answer the questions.

ES

a Rotate the triangle shown 180° about the point (1, 2).

b Write down the co-ordinates of each of the vertices of your rotated triangle.

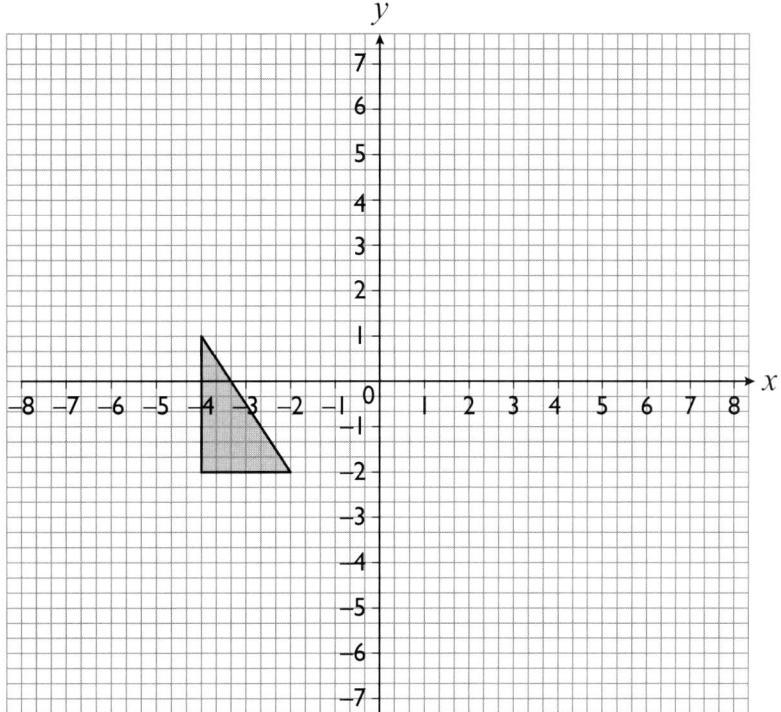

PS 5 Copy the diagram and answer the questions.

ES

a Rotate the triangle shown 90° anticlockwise about the point (–1, 2).

b Write down the co-ordinates of each of the vertices of your rotated triangle.

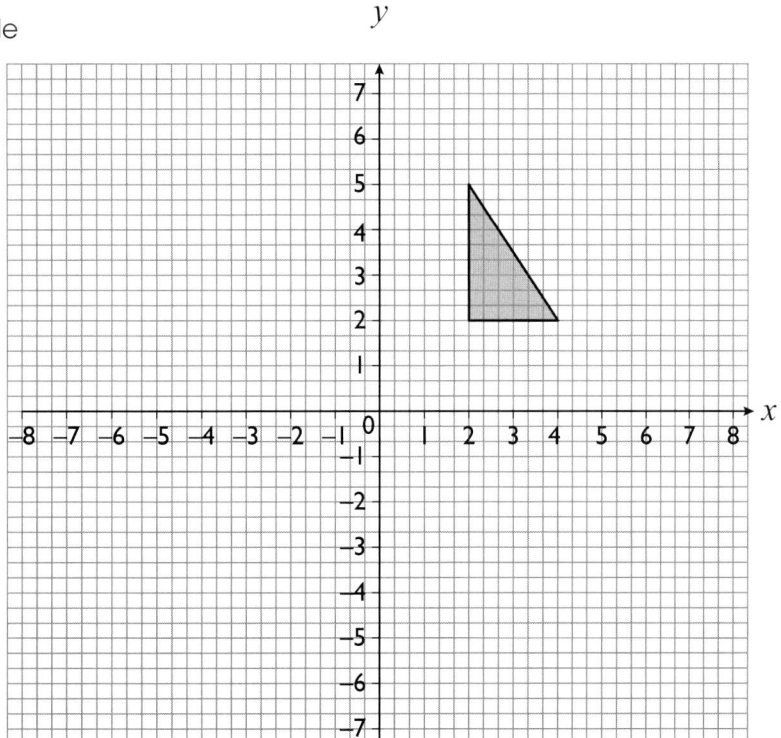

107

PS **6** Copy the diagram and answer the questions.

ES

a Rotate the triangle shown 90° anticlockwise about the point (−3, −2).

b Write down the co-ordinates of each of the vertices of your rotated triangle.

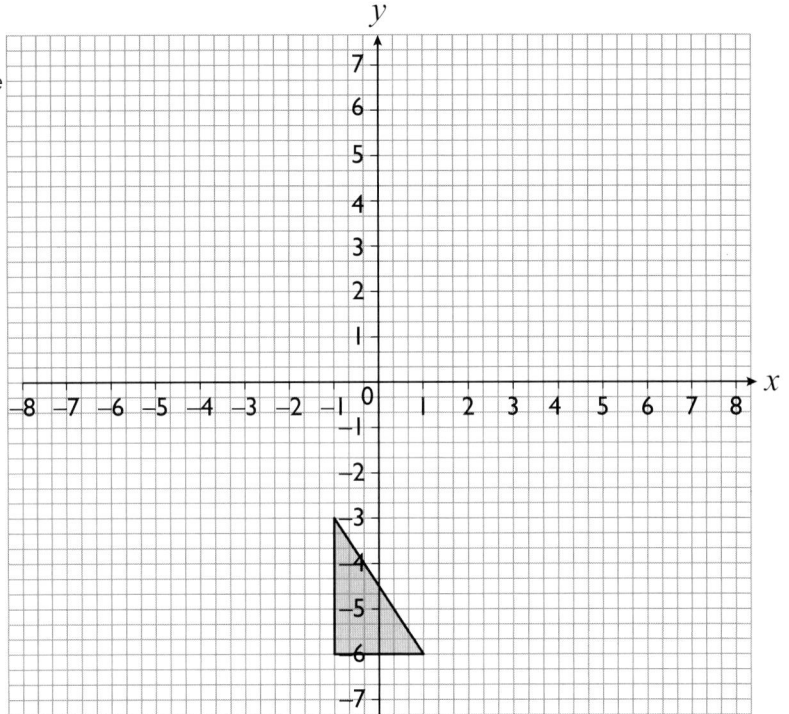

PS **7** Copy the diagram and answer the questions.

ES

a Rotate the triangle shown 90° anticlockwise about the point (−2, 1).

b Write down the co-ordinates of each of the vertices of your rotated triangle.

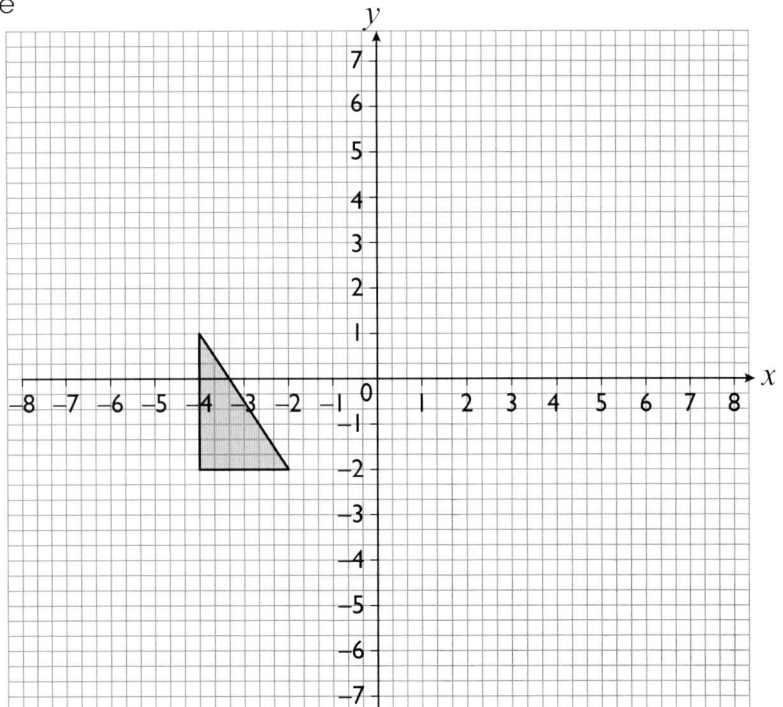

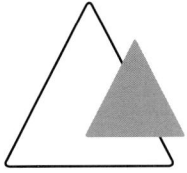

Geometry and Measures
Strand 5 Transformations
Unit 6 Enlargement

PS — PRACTISING SKILLS   DF — DEVELOPING FLUENCY   PB — PROBLEM SOLVING   ES — EXAM-STYLE

PS 1 Here is a grid of squares.

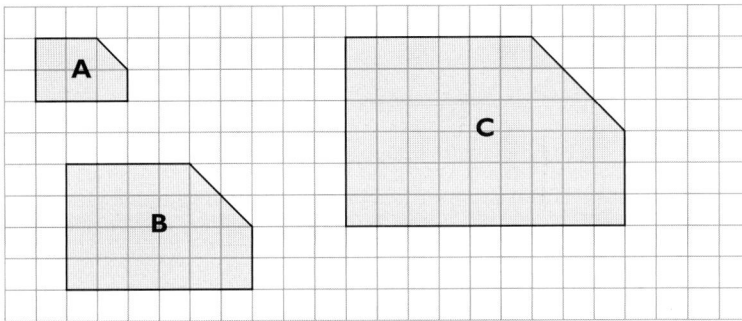

Write down the scale factor of the enlargement that takes

a A to B

b A to C

c B to C.

PS 2 Enlarge these shapes by scale factor 2. Use the cross marked nearest the shape as the centre of enlargement.

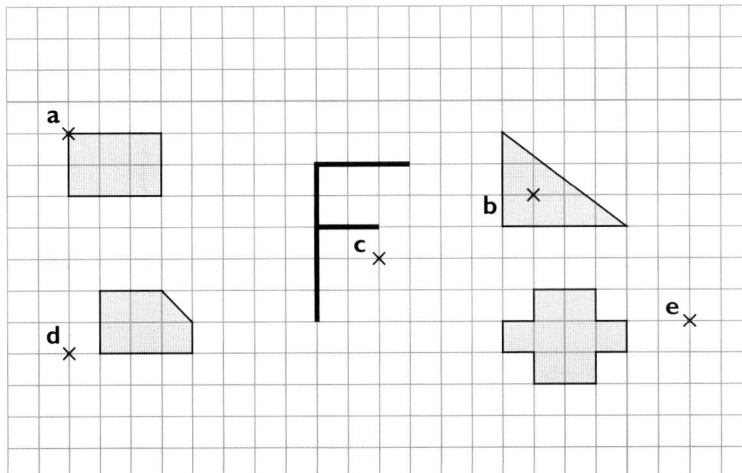

DF **PB**

3 Enlarge triangle P by

   a scale factor 2 centre (–1, 0)

   b scale factor 3 centre (–4, 2).

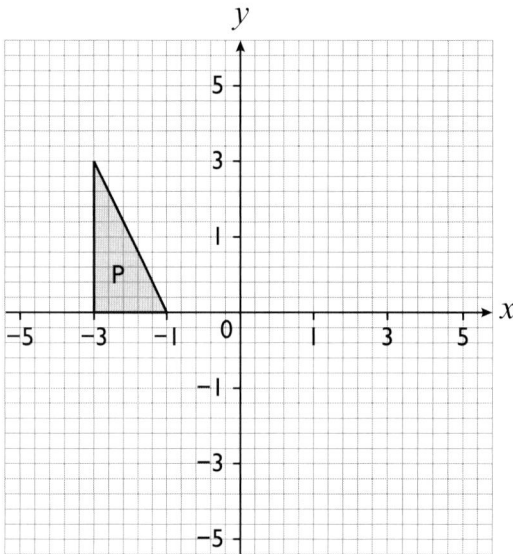

DF **PB**

4 Make three copies of this diagram. Enlarge triangle T by

   a scale factor 3 centre (4, 3)

   b scale factor 2 centre (2, 2)

   c scale factor 1.5 centre (3, 1).

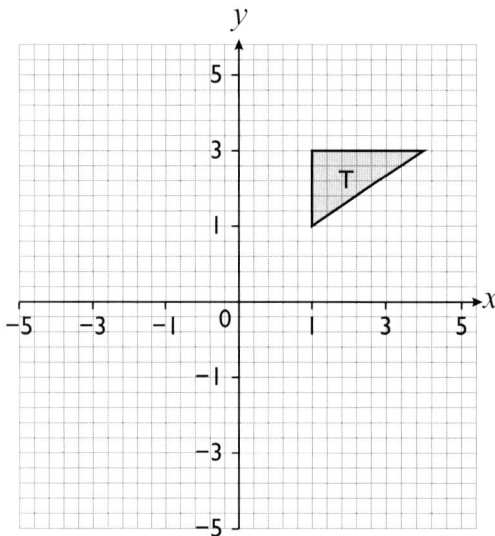

DF **5** Describe fully the single transformation that maps

    a triangle T onto triangle Q

    b triangle T onto triangle R.

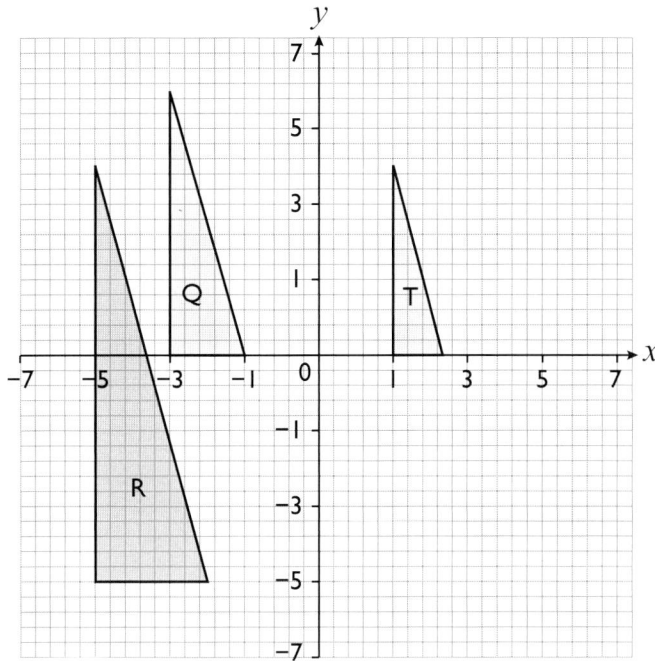

PB **6** Here is a small photograph. The small photograph is enlarged by
ES scale factor 3 to make a large photograph.

    What is the perimeter of the large photograph?

PB
ES

7 Here is a photograph. Jill makes enlargements of the photograph.

6 cm

8 cm

Enlargement A

32 cm

Enlargement B

16 cm

a Find the scale factor of the enlargement of Enlargement A.

b Find the width of Enlargement A.

c Work out the perimeter of Enlargement B.

PB
ES

8 Dilys has a picture she wants to put into a photograph frame. The photograph has a length of 5 cm and a width of 3 cm. The photograph frame has a length of 17.5 cm. She is going to enlarge the photograph to fit in the frame.

What width does the frame have to be to fit in the enlarged photograph?

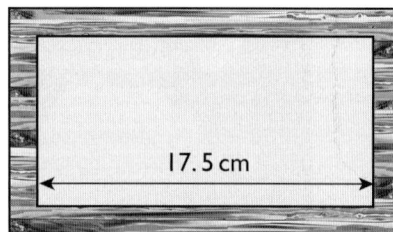

3 cm

5 cm

17.5 cm

DF **9** Enlarge triangle P by

   a scale factor $\frac{1}{2}$ centre (–4, 4)

   b scale factor $\frac{1}{3}$ centre (–4, –5).

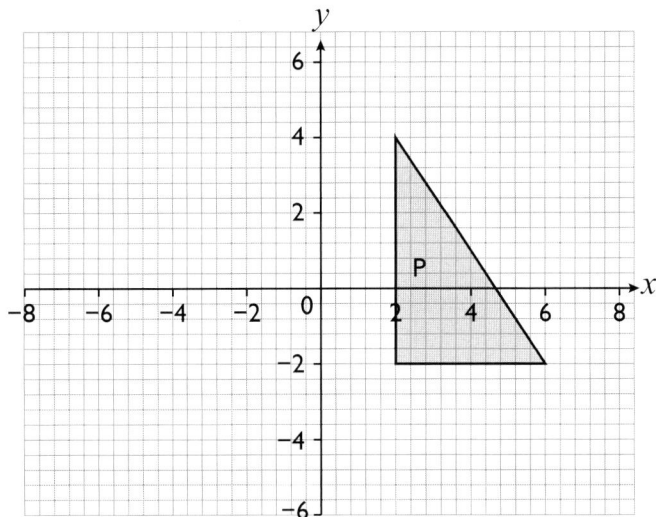

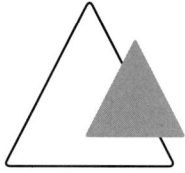

PS **1** Here is the net of a 3-D solid.

ES   **a** Write down the name of the solid.

    b Draw a 3-D sketch of the solid.

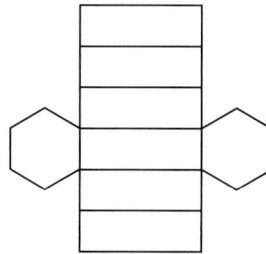

PS **2** Here is a 3-D shape.

ES   **a** Write down the name of the shape.

    b Draw the net of the shape.

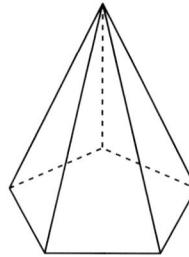

DF **3** Here is 3-D shape.

    a Write down the name of the shape.

    b Write down the number of

      i edges

      ii vertices

      iii faces.

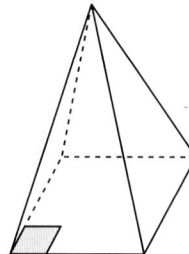

PB **4** Here is the net of a cube. There is a cross
ES marked at one of the vertices. When the net
is made into a cube which other corner
meets the one marked with the cross?

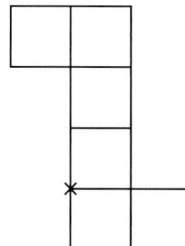

PB **ES** **5** The diagram shows a box for chocolates.
The box is in the shape of a triangular prism.
Draw an accurate net for the box.

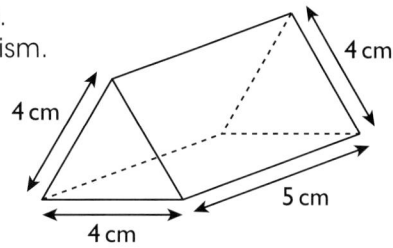

4 cm

4 cm

4 cm

5 cm

DF **ES** **6** A box is in the shape of a cuboid with
length 5 cm
width 3 cm
height 2 cm.
Draw an accurate net of the cuboid.

PB **ES** **7** A chocolate bar is in the shape of a triangular prism. A paper wrapper
covers the three rectangular faces of the chocolate bar. There is a 1 cm
additional flap on the wrapper.
Work out the length of the wrapper.

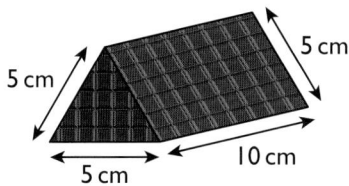

5 cm

5 cm

5 cm

10 cm

Wrapper

DF **8** A cube has 6 different faces.
Draw a net to show the faces in their position on the cube.

PB **9** Idris fixes a ribbon to the top corner P of a cuboid and the bottom
corner Q of the cuboid. PQR is a straight line.
Find, by drawing, the length of the ribbon PQR.

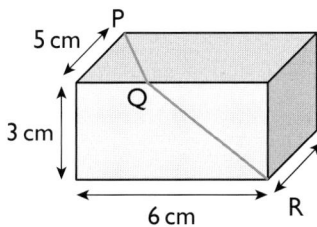

P

5 cm

Q

3 cm

6 cm

R

Geometry and Measures Strand 6 Three-dimensional shapes Unit 3 Volume and surface area of cuboids

PS — **PRACTISING SKILLS**   **DF** — **DEVELOPING FLUENCY**   **PB** — **PROBLEM SOLVING**   **ES** — **EXAM-STYLE**

PS **1** Work out the volume of these cuboids.   ●○○

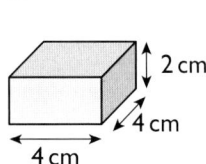

a

2 cm, 4 cm, 4 cm

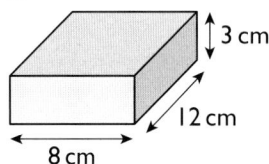

b

3 cm, 12 cm, 8 cm

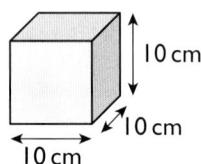

c

10 cm, 10 cm, 10 cm

PS **2** Work out the surface area of these cuboids.   ●○○

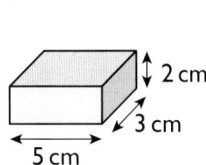

a

2 cm, 3 cm, 5 cm

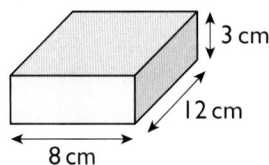

b

3 cm, 12 cm, 8 cm

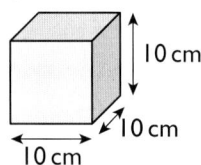

c

10 cm, 10 cm, 10 cm

DF **3** **a** A cube has a volume of 27 cm³. Find its surface area.   ●○○

ES **b** A cube has a surface area of 96 cm². Find its volume.   ●○○

PB **4** Here is diagram of a carton that contains one litre of orange juice.   ●○○
ES The base of the container is a square of side 8 cm.
Find the least height of the container.

Orange Juice 1 litre

1 litre = 1000 cm³

DF
ES
5 Dylan has a box of toy bricks. Each toy brick is a cube with side 5 cm.
The box is full of toy bricks.
What is the greatest number of toy bricks that can fit into the box?

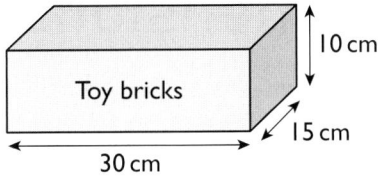

Toy bricks
10 cm
15 cm
30 cm

DF
ES
6 Tea is sold in boxes. The boxes are 12 cm tall. The base is a square
of side 5 cm. The boxes of tea are delivered to shops in cartons. The
cartons are cuboids with length 60 cm, width 30 cm and height 36 cm.
Work out the greatest number of boxes of tea will fit into a carton.

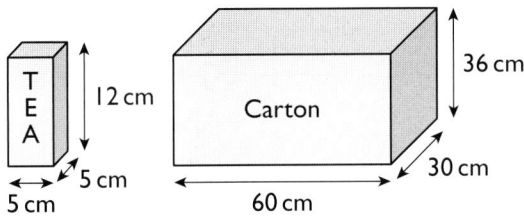

T
E
A
12 cm
5 cm
5 cm
Carton
36 cm
30 cm
60 cm

PB
ES
7 An oil tank is in the shape of a cuboid.
The oil tank is 2.5 m by 1.5 m by 60 cm.

a Find the volume of the oil tank.

The oil tank is half full of oil.

b How much oil needs to be added to
the tank to fill it completely?

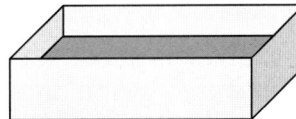

$1 m^3 = 1000$ litres

PB
ES
8 Owain is going to paint his swimming pool. The pool stands on flat
ground and is in the shape of a cuboid. He is going to paint the four
outside faces and all the inside faces.

The pool has dimensions 15 m by 8 m by 1.2 m. The paint Owain is going
to use covers 15 m^2 with 1 litre of paint.
How many litres of paint will Owain need to buy?

PB
9 Delyth designs a box with a lid. The box is to hold wooden discs which
have a radius of 6 cm and a height of 0.5 cm. Delyth's box has to hold
up to 120 discs.
Work out the dimensions of a box that Delyth could use.

PB
ES
10 Catrin has a shed with a flat roof. The roof is a rectangle with length
1.8 m and width 1.2 m. One night 2.5 cm of rain fell on the roof and
was collected in a container that is in the shape of a cuboid.

The container has a height of 1.5 m and has a square base of
side 30 cm. At the beginning of the night there was 10 cm of rain
in the container.

Work out the height of the water in the container at the end of
the night.

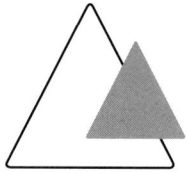

Geometry and Measures Strand 6 Three-dimensional shapes Unit 4 2-D representations of 3-D shapes

PS — PRACTISING SKILLS   **DF** — DEVELOPING FLUENCY   **PB** — PROBLEM SOLVING   **ES** — EXAM-STYLE

PB **1** Here is a 3-D drawing of Graham's garage. The front face and back face are rectangles. The other two vertical faces are trapeziums.

On squared paper, using a scale of 1 cm to represent 1 m

a draw a plan of the garage

b draw the front elevation of the garage

c draw the side elevation of the garage from the direction shown by the arrow.

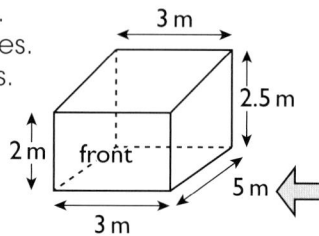

DF **2** Here are some mathematical shapes. They have all got square bases of side 5 cm. On squared paper sketch for each shape

a the plan

b the front elevation

c the side elevation.

8 cm

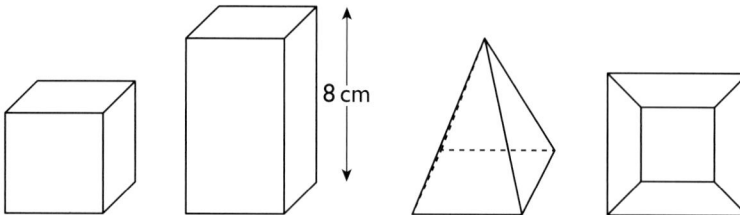

PS **ES** **3** Here are the plan, front elevation and side elevation of a 3-D shape. Draw a sketch of the 3-D shape.

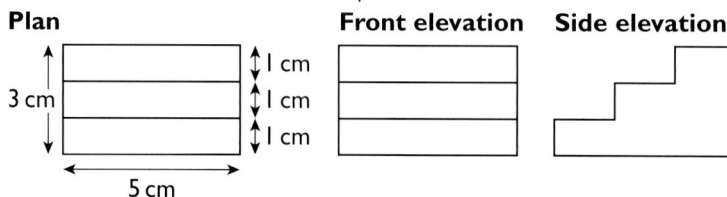

Plan   3 cm   1 cm   1 cm   1 cm   5 cm

Front elevation

Side elevation

DF
ES
4 Here are the plan, front elevation and side elevation of a shape that ⬤⬤○
has been made from centimetre cubes.

Draw a sketch of the 3-D solid made from these cubes.
Use isometric paper.

Plan   **Front elevation**   **Side elevation**

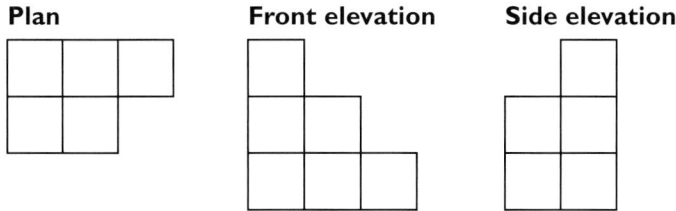

DF **5** Here is a shape made from a cuboid and a triangular prism. The ⬤⬤○
cuboid has dimensions 6 cm by 4 cm by 4 cm. The triangular prism
has a square base and has a height of 6 cm.

a Draw the plan and front elevation for the 3-D shape.

b Draw the side elevations from the direction of

   i the black arrow

   ii the white arrow.

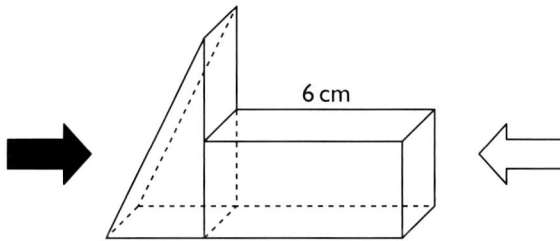

6 cm

DF
ES
6 Here are the plan, front and side elevation of a 3-D shape. ⬤⬤○
Draw a sketch of the 3-D shape.

Plan

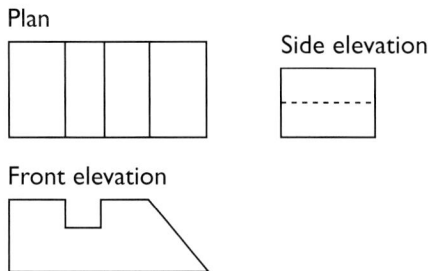

Side elevation

Front elevation

PB
ES
7 Here is a drawing of Sid's shed. ⬤⬤○
The shed is made from 4 vertical walls
and a rectangular sloping roof.

a Draw the side elevation of the shed. 2.5 m

b Find the area of the roof of the shed.

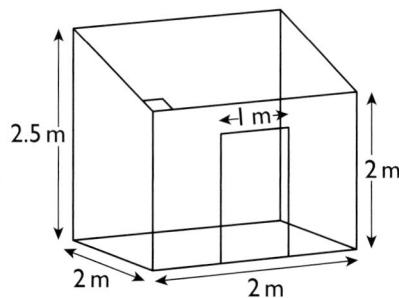

1 m

2 m

2 m   2 m

119

Statistics and Probability
Strand 1 Statistical measures
Unit 3 Using frequency tables

PS PRACTISING SKILLS   DF DEVELOPING FLUENCY   PB PROBLEM SOLVING   ES EXAM-STYLE

PS 1 Betty recorded the number of marks some students achieved in a test. Here are her results.

Number of marks	Frequency
7	4
8	14
9	8
10	6

  a How many students did the test?

  b Write down the mode.

  c Find the median.

  d Work out the mean.

PS 2 A taxi driver recorded the number of people he carried for each of 30 fares. Here are his results.

Number of people	Frequency
1	15
2	9
3	6

  a Write down the mode.

  b Find the median.

  c Work out the total number of people carried.

  d Work out the mean.

DF 3 Here are the numbers of eggs in each of 29 sparrow's nests.

2	3	5	5	3	5	2	4	5	4
3	4	4	2	4	3	5	5	4	4
4	3	5	4	4	3	3	2	5	

  a Construct a frequency table for this data.

  b Draw a bar chart for your frequency table.

  c Write down the mode.

  d Work out the mean. Give your answer correct to 2 decimal places.

DF **4** Hoeg sells shirts. The table gives information about the shirts he sold on Friday and on Saturday.

Collar size	Frequency on Friday	Frequency on Saturday
14	4	0
$14\frac{1}{2}$	7	9
15	17	15
$15\frac{1}{2}$	32	28
16	30	37
$16\frac{1}{2}$	16	19

a On which day did Hoeg sell the most shirts?

b For each day
  i write down the mode
  ii find the range.

c Compare the modes and the ranges for these two days.

d Construct a frequency table for the data for Friday and Saturday combined.

e Use your frequency table to find the median collar size for the combined data.

DF
ES **5** The bar chart gives information about the numbers of letters Fritz received on each of 25 days.

a Construct a frequency table for this information.

b Work out the total number of letters Fritz got.

c Work out the mean number of letters each day.

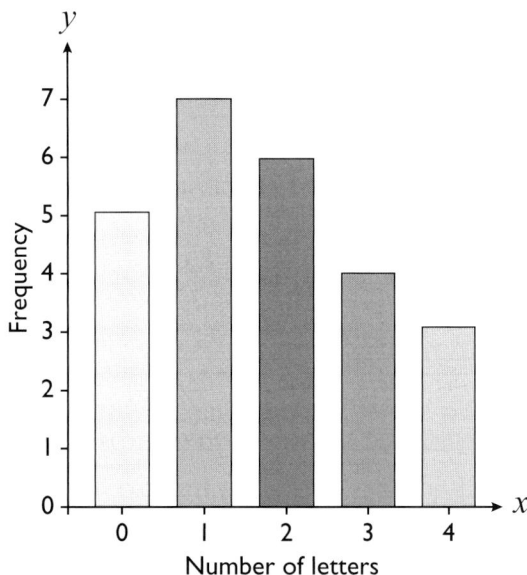

PB
ES

6 75 males and 75 females were asked to rate a film on a score
of 1 to 5. A score of 5 represents the highest rating. Here are the results.

Male	
Score	Frequency
1	5
2	11
3	22
4	29
5	8

Female	
Score	Frequency
1	2
2	15
3	19
4	35
5	4

a Find the mode, median and mean for the males and for
the females.

b Sam says: 'On average the males liked the film more than
the females.' Is she right? Give a reason for your answer.

PB
ES

7 The stem and leaf diagram shows information about the
weights, in grams, of a sample of bats. The bats in the sample
are all the same species.

```
2 | 4  6  9
3 | 0  I  2  4  4  4  4  7  8
4 | 3  5  6  6  7  9
5 | 2  4
```

Key: 2 | 4 represents 24 grams

a Write down the modal weight.

b Work out the range of the weights.

The mean weight of a bottle-nose bat is 40 grams.

c Do you think the bats in the sample are bottle-nosed bats?
Explain your answer.

PB
ES

8 Naveed records the numbers of books of stamps he sells.
On Monday he sold:

   1 book of stamps to each of 8 people

   2 books of stamps to each of 14 people

   3 books of stamps to each of 23 people.

Naveed also sold 4 books of stamps to a number of other people
and kept a record. He can't read what he recorded. He knows
he sold a total of 125 books of stamps on Monday.

Work out the number of people he sold 4 books of stamps to.

PB **9** Bryn is the manager of a coffee shop. The table gives some information about the drinks he sold on Thursday.

Drink	Cost	Frequency
Coffee	£2.99	62
Tea	£1.99	49
Orange squash	£1.25	25
Orange juice	£2.49	12
Blackcurrant juice	£1.25	20

a Work out the range of the costs.

Bryn makes a profit if the total amount he gets from drinks is greater than £200.

b Does Bryn make a profit? How much profit?

c Work out the mean cost of a drink.

Bryn thinks that he will sell more than 250 drinks on Friday.

d Find an estimate for the least amount of money he expects to earn on drinks sold on Friday.

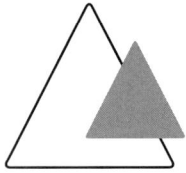

Statistics and Probability
Strand 2 Statistical diagrams
Unit 5 Scatter diagrams

PS — PRACTISING SKILLS   DF — DEVELOPING FLUENCY   PB — PROBLEM SOLVING   ES — EXAM-STYLE

DF **PB** **1** The scatter diagram shows the takings at the entrance to a castle and the number of visitors.

    a How much where the takings on the day when there were most visitors, the busiest day at the castle?

    b Carys says Sunday was the busiest day at the castle. Is Carys correct? You must give a reason for your answer.

    c Use the idea of a line of best fit, or otherwise, to estimate the takings when there are 95 visitors to the castle.

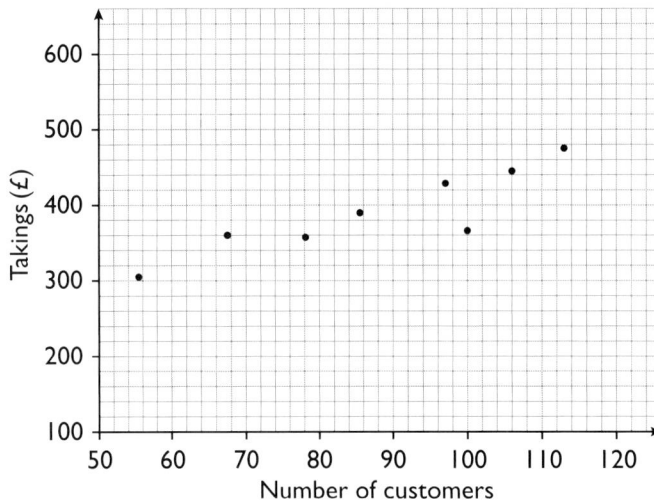

DF **PB** **2** Gwilym runs the coffee shop in a large department store. He has drawn a scatter diagram to show takings and number of customers.

    a Describe the correlation.

    b On one day the coffee shop took £430. How many customers were there on that day?

    c How much on average did each customer spend in the coffee shop? Show your workings.

d Considering a line of best fit, or otherwise, if the coffee shop takes £450 in one day, about how many customers would there be?

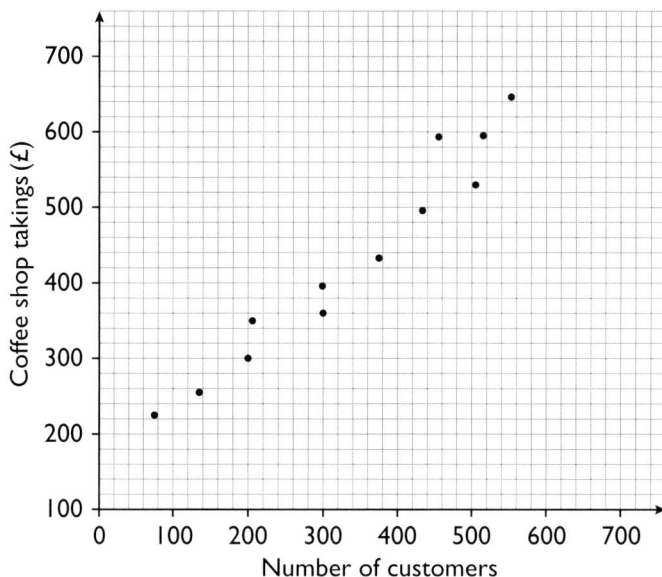

PS
ES
3 Gwen has measured the length and width of some leaves from a tree in her garden. She draws a scatter diagram to show the results.

a What is the length of the widest leaf Gwen measured?

b What is the width of the longest leaf Gwen measured?

c Describe the correlation seen in the scatter diagram.

d Would it be reasonable that another leaf that Gwen measures has a length that is double its width? Give a reason for your answer.

e Considering a line of best fit, or otherwise, what might be the length of a leaf from this same tree that has a width of 2 cm?

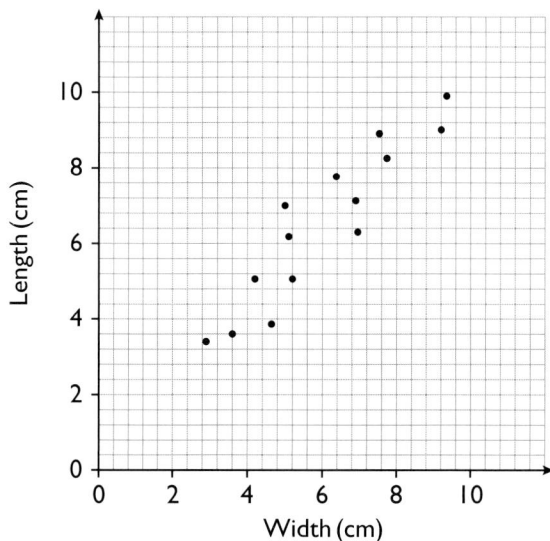

PS **ES** **4** Rhys has measured the length and width of some leaves from his garden. He draws a scatter diagram to show the results.

a There is no correlation in the results. Why might this be?

b What is the width of the shortest leaf measured?

c One leaf has a length that is double its width. Write down the length and width of this leaf.

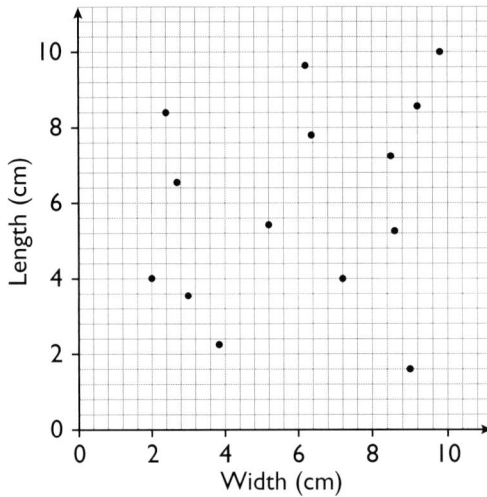

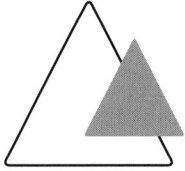

Statistics and Probability
Strand 2 Statistical diagrams
Unit 6 Using lines of best fit

PS — PRACTISING SKILLS   DF — DEVELOPING FLUENCY   PB — PROBLEM SOLVING   ES — EXAM-STYLE

DF **1** Dewi has drawn a scatter diagram to show the rental prices of some
PB one-bedroom flats and the distance the flat is from the city centre.   ● ● ●

    a One of the flats is an outlier. How far is this flat from the centre and what is its rental price?

    b On a copy of this scatter diagram, draw a line of best fit. Are there any points you have ignored in drawing your line of best fit? *(Or you may use tracing paper over the scatter in the book, then show your teacher your line of best fit.)*

    c What might you expect the rental price to be for a one-bedroom flat that is 1.75 km from the city centre?

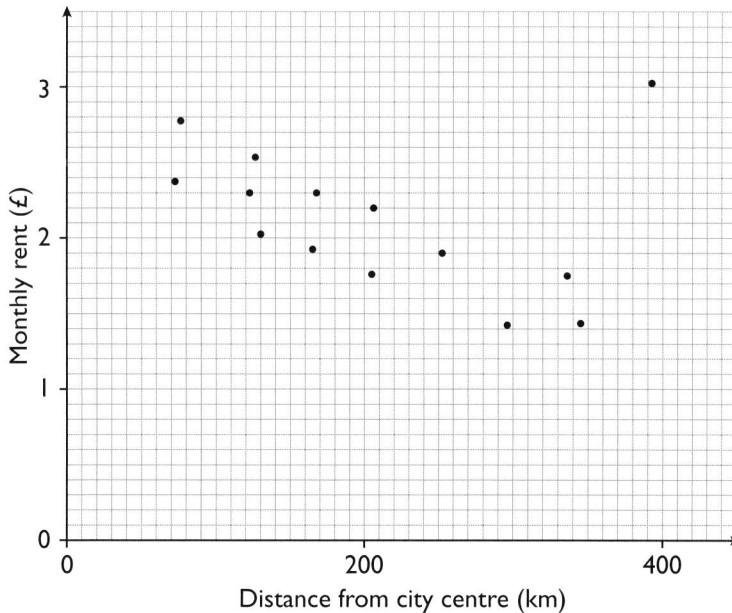

DF
PB

2 Rhian works for a museum. Entrance to the museum is free, but all visitors are asked for a donation towards the upkeep of the museum. Rhian has recorded the number of visitors and the total donations made on each day for a week.

Number of visitors	55	25	30	42	34	46	26
Total donation (£)	100	45	60	80	66	90	50

a Use axes like those shown below, to draw a scatter diagram for these results.

b Is it possible to say how many visitors there were on Tuesday? Give a reason for your answer.

c Draw a line of best fit, by eye, on your scatter diagram.

d Use your line of best fit to estimate the total donation that may be made if there were 50 visitors to the museum.

e Rhian says that the results show that the museum will always receive a donation of approximately £2 per visitor. Is this completely true? You must give a reason for your answer.

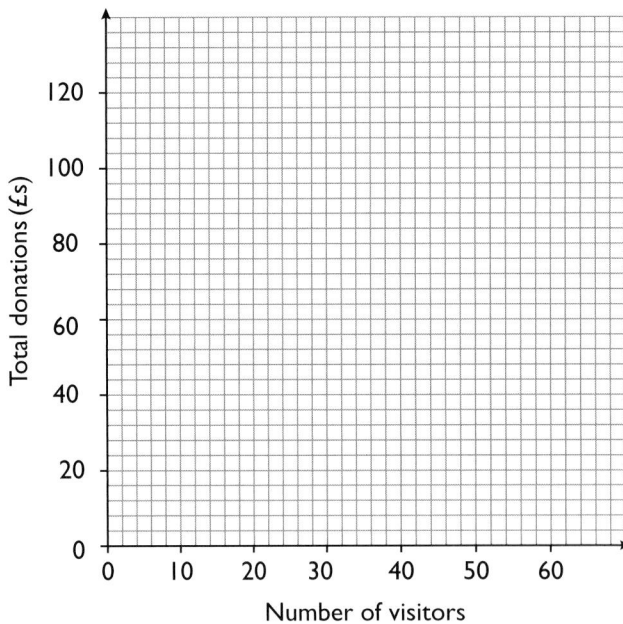

PS
ES
3 Tomos has been measuring and recording the length and mass of a certain type of worm. Here is his table of results.

Length (mm)	10	12	22	6	11	16	17	9	8	14
Mass (g)	2.0	2.5	4.3	1.4	2.4	3.4	3.2	1.8	1.6	3.0

a Use graph paper to draw and label suitable axes to represent this data in a scatter diagram.

b What sort of correlation does your scatter diagram show?

c Calculate the mean length and the mean mass of these 10 worms.

d Draw a line of best fit on your scatter diagram.

e Use your line of best fit to estimate the mass of a worm of this type with a length of 2 cm.

f Use your line of best fit to estimate the mass of each 3 cm length of this type of worm.

PS
ES
4 The scatter diagram shows the takings at the entrance to a castle and the number of visitors.

a Calculate the mean takings and the mean number of visitors.

b On a copy of this scatter diagram, or using tracing paper over this diagram, draw a line of best fit.

c Write down the number of visitors and takings for the extra point you plotted in part **b**.

d Lois says, 'If the number of visitors was 300 one day, we might expect to take approximately £1500.'

　　i Make a better estimate for the takings if there were 300 visitors to the castle one day.

　　ii Why might even your better estimate be unreasonable?

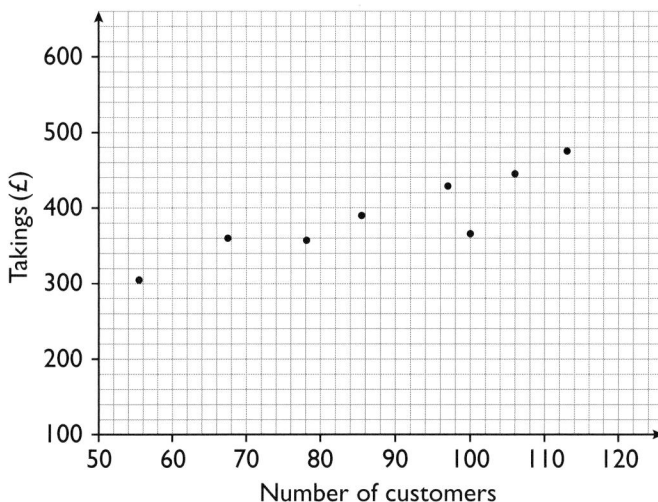

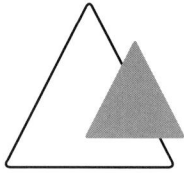

Statistics and Probability
Strand 3 Collecting data Unit 2
Designing questionnaires

PS PRACTISING SKILLS   DF DEVELOPING FLUENCY   PB PROBLEM SOLVING   ES EXAM-STYLE

DF PB **1** A medical centre is carrying out a survey to encourage patients to eat five portions of fruit or vegetables a day. Here is a section from the survey.

Do you eat 5 portions of fruit or vegetables?

Yes ☐
No ☐
Occasionally ☐

a Write a criticism of the question.

b Write a criticism of the response options.

c Write a suitable question that could be asked and give appropriate response boxes.

DF PB **2** Write a question, with a selection of answer boxes, to find out peoples' single favourite sandwich filling.

DF PB **3** Lois is conducting a survey to find out the views of local people about the council's policy on recycling garden waste. She asks people in the town centre one Tuesday morning at 12 noon. Here are the first two questions.

1	How much garden waste do you have each week?
2	Do you agree that the council should charge for the collection of garden waste?

Make 3 criticisms of Lois's survey.

PS DF **4** 'People brushing their teeth 3 times a day have fewer fillings.'

a Do you think this is a reasonable hypothesis? Give a reason for you answer.

b How would you test this hypothesis?

PS
ES

5 Bryn wanted to find out if people supported the local rugby team.
He carried out a survey outside the local rugby club before a game.
Here is his questionnaire.

1	How old are you?
	16 to 20 ☐
	20 to 30 ☐
	30 to 40 ☐
	Over 40 ☐
2	How often do you come to rugby games?
	Never ☐
	Sometimes ☐
	Often ☐
3	Do you support this rugby club?
	Yes ☐
	No ☐

  a Explain why Bryn's survey could be biased.

  b Write down a criticism of each question in the questionnaire.

  c Rewrite the questionnaire to improve it, addressing all your criticisms.

6 'People are involved in more accidents walking in the street if they
text as they walk through the street than if they don't.'

  a Do you think this is a reasonable hypothesis? Give a reason for you answer.

  b How would you test this hypothesis? Write any questions you may be asking.

131

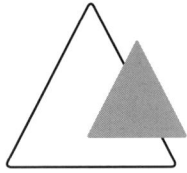

Statistics and Probability
Strand 4 Probability Unit 2
Single event probability

PS ─ PRACTISING SKILLS   **DF** ─ DEVELOPING FLUENCY   **PB** ─ PROBLEM SOLVING   **ES** ─ EXAM-STYLE

PS **1** Here are some cards. Each card has a shape drawn on it. Stephanie is going to take one of the cards at random.

    a Which shape has the greater probability of being taken, an arrow or a heart? Give a reason for your answer.

    b Write down the probability that the shape will be an arrow.

PS **2** Jasmine rolls a biased die. The probability that the die will land on a 6 is 0.4.

Work out the probability that the die will not land on a 6.

PS **3** There are 3 red counters, 2 green counters and 6 yellow counters in a bag. Yuan is going to take, at random, a counter from the bag.

    a What is the probability that the counter will be

       i red

       ii green

       iii yellow

       iv white?

    b What is the probability the counter will **not** be

       i red

       ii green

       iii yellow

       iv white?

DF **4** The probability of event A is $\frac{1}{3}$. The probability of event B is 0.35.

The probability of event C is 30%.

Write these events in order of likelihood. Start with the least likely event.

DF **5** The vertical line chart shows the flavours and numbers of sweets in a box. Maja is going to take, at random, a sweet from the box.

a Which flavour of sweet has the smallest probability of being taken?

b Write down the probability that the flavour will be
  i strawberry
  ii lime.

c Write down the probability that the flavour will not be
  i orange
  ii lemon.

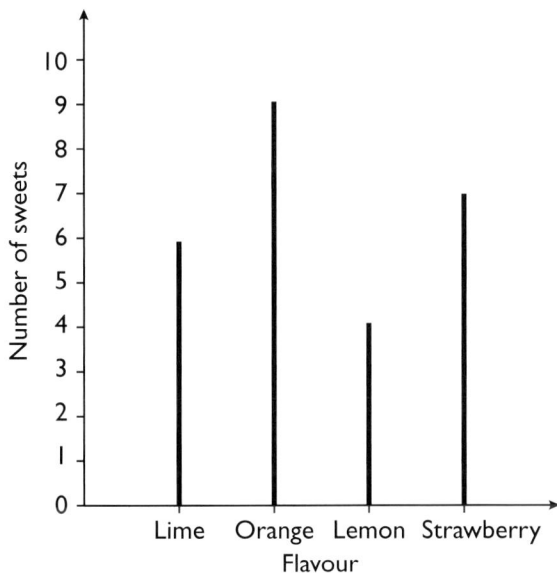

DF **6** The pie chart gives information about the ages of the people watching a film at a cinema.

One of these people is picked at random. Find the probability that the age of this person will be

a 51 years and over

b 50 years or less

c 31–50 years

d 11–30 years.

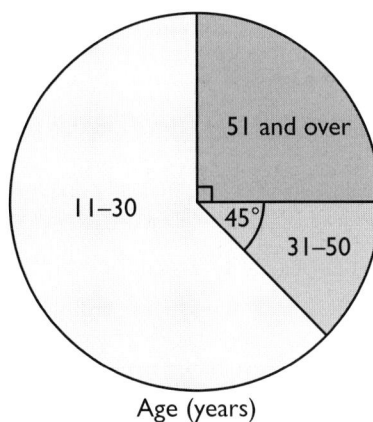

DF **7** The stem and leaf diagram gives the number of people on each of 25 tours.

1	7 7 8 9 9 9
2	1 2 3 3 3 4 4 6 6 6 8 9 9
3	0 0 1 2 2 3

Key: 1|7 represents 17 people

Henry picks, at random, one of these tours. What is the probability that this tour has on it

a exactly 26 people

b 19 people or less

c more than 25 people

d between 20 and 25 people?

PB **8** Nesta is designing a fair spinner to use in her probability lessons. She is going to spin the spinner once.

Copy and complete the spinner for each question. You must only use letters A, B and C.

Write 4 letters on the spinner so that it is

a more likely to get an A than a B

b equally likely to get an A or a C

c twice as likely to get a B than an A.

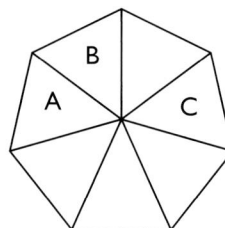

PB **ES** **9** Box A contains 3 bags of ready salted crisps and 4 bags of cheese and onion crisps. Box B contains 4 bags of ready salted crisps and 7 bags of cheese and onion crisps.

Tiny is going to take, at random, a bag of crisps from one of the boxes. She wants to have the best chance of taking a bag of ready salted crisps.

Which box should she use? Explain why.

PB **ES** **10** Silvia is designing a probability experiment. She puts 15 green counters and 35 blue counters in a bag.

a What is probability of taking, at random, a green counter from the bag?

Silvia puts some more blue counters in the bag. The probability of taking at random a green counter from the bag is now 0.25.

b How many blue counters did she put in the bag?

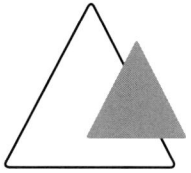

Statistics and Probability
Strand 4 Probability Unit 3
Combined events

PS PRACTISING SKILLS   DF DEVELOPING FLUENCY   PB PROBLEM SOLVING   ES EXAM-STYLE

PS 1 Nathalie spins three fair coins. Here are the possible outcomes.

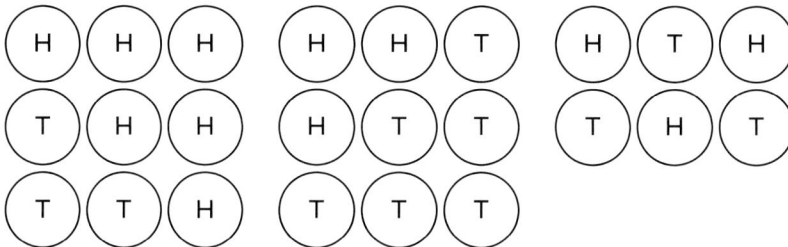

(H)(H)(H) (H)(H)(T) (H)(T)(H)

(T)(H)(H) (H)(T)(T) (T)(H)(T)

(T)(T)(H) (T)(T)(T)

Write down the probability that she will get

a 3 heads

b one head and two tails

c two heads and a tail

d at least two heads.

PS 2 Simon goes to a restaurant. He can choose from three types of soup and from three types of bread.

Soup	Bread
Tomato	Brown
Vegetable	White
Lentil	Granary

Simon is going to choose one type of soup and one type of bread.

a List all the possible combinations Simon can choose.

Simon chooses, at random, one type of bread.

b Write down the probability that he will choose Granary.

PS 3 Here are some letters and some numbers on cards.

| A | B | C | | 2 | 3 | 4 | 5 |

Safta is going to take, at random, one of the cards with a letter on it and one of the cards with a number on it.

a One possible combination is (A, 2). Write down all the other possible combinations.

b Write down the probability he will take

  i (A, 2)

  ii B and any number

  iii C and a prime number

  iv A or C and an even number.

DF 4 Wilhelm spins a fair 5-sided spinner and a fair 4-sided spinner.

	1	2	3	4
1	2	3	4	5
2	3	4		
3	4			
4				
5				

a Copy and complete the table to show all the possible total scores.

b What is the probability that the total score is

  i exactly 9

  ii exactly 7

  iii an odd number

  iv 4 or less.

DF 5 There are 50 students in a college. Each student may study Polish, Welsh and Chinese.

The Venn diagram gives information about the numbers of students studying all, two, one, or none of these languages.

One of the 50 students is picked at random.

a What is the probability that this student studies

  i all three languages

  ii only Polish

  iii both Chinese and Welsh

  iv Chinese?

One of the 17 students studying Welsh is picked at random.

b What is the probability that this student also studies

   i Chinese

   ii both Chinese and Polish?

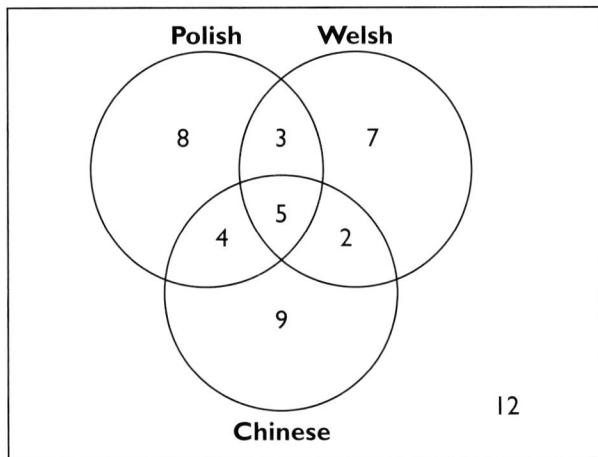

PB **ES** **6** Hoeg asked 59 people at a youth club if they play tennis or squash.
35 people said they play tennis. 28 people said they play squash.
17 people said they play both tennis and squash.

   a Copy and complete the Venn diagram.

One of these people is picked at random.

   b Find the probability that this person plays

     i squash

     ii tennis, but not squash

     iii tennis or squash, but not both

     iv neither tennis nor squash.

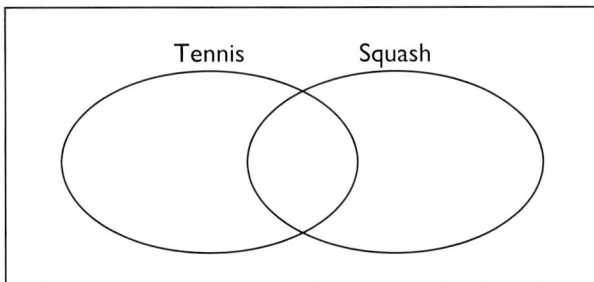

PB **7** Oparbi asked some children which of three films they like the best. The incomplete table shows some information about her results.

	Minions	Inside out	Wall·E	Total
Boys	14	A	8	B
Girls	C	5	D	21
Total	20	E	F	47

a Find the missing values A–F.

One of these children is picked at random.

b What is the probability that this child will be

i a boy

ii a girl who likes *Minions* the best.

One of the girls is picked at random.

c What is the probability that this girl likes *Wall·E* the best?

PB **8** 130 students were each asked to choose an activity for a school trip.
ES The table gives information about these students and the activity they chose.

	Cinema	Theatre	Concert
Male	28	17	14
Female	32	23	16

One of the students is picked at random.

a Find the probability that this student

i is male

ii is a female who chose concert

iii is a male who did not choose cinema.

One of the male students is picked at random.

b Find the probability that this student

i chose theatre

ii did not choose concert.

PB **9** Here are some cards. Each card has a letter on it. Nerys takes, at random, two of the cards.

a Write down all the possible combinations.

b What is the probability that one of these two cards has S on it?

Jim takes, at random, three of the cards.

c Write down all the possible combinations.

d What is the probability that one of these three cards has S on it?

C	A	R	D	S

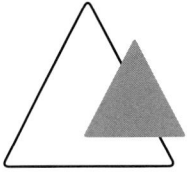

Statistics and Probability
Strand 4 Probability Unit 4
Estimating probability

PS — PRACTISING SKILLS   DF — DEVELOPING FLUENCY   PB — PROBLEM SOLVING   ES — EXAM-STYLE

DF PB ES **1** An eight-sided dice has the numbers 1 to 8 on it. The dice is thrown 20 times and the number it lands on is recorded.

1	3	4	5	6	1	2	2	7	3
2	5	7	8	4	5	4	2	1	6

    a Copy and complete the frequency table. Write the relative frequencies as decimals.

    b Find the probability that the dice will land on an even number less than 5.

    c Find the probability that the dice will land on a number greater than 7.

Lands on	1	2	3	4	5	6	7	8
Number of times								
Relative frequency								

PS DF PB ES **2** A shop sells 4 different types of milk. Here are the sales for the week.

Types of milk	Full fat	Semi skimmed	Skimmed	Soya
Sales (litres)	24	26	40	10

    a Estimate that the next litre of milk sold will be semi skimmed.

    b A new superstore in the area estimates it will sell 450 litres of milk each day. How many litres of each type of milk would you suggest the new superstore should stock each day?

PS DF PB ES **3** A school conducts a survey to see if students think the dining area should be open at break time to sell breakfast. Here are the results.

Decision	Frequency
Yes	340
No	160
No opinion	100

a Use the data to estimate the probability that a student selected randomly will answer:

   i yes

   ii no

   iii no opinion.

b The management of the school have already decided to not open the dining area at break time to sell breakfast if less than 40% of the pupils answered 'yes'. Will the management of the school decision be to open the dining area to sell breakfast or not? You must support your answer with a suitable calculation.

4 A five-sided spinner has the numbers 2, 4, 6, 8 and 10 on it. The table shows the probability of it landing on some of the numbers.

Number	2	4	6	8	10
Probability	0.21	0.25	0.18		

a The probability that the spinner lands on 10 is double that of it landing on 8. Complete the table.

b Alwena spins the spinner 250 times.

   i How many times would you expect Alwena to to get a 6?

   ii How many times would you expect Alwena **not** to get a 6?

5 Ms Evans measures the heights of the girls and boys in her tutor group. She records her results in a table.

Height (cm)	Less than 160cm	160cm	Greater than 160cm
Number of girls	6	2	9
Number of boys	0	3	10

a A pupil from Ms Evans tutor group is selected at random. Calculate the probability that the pupil selected is

   i a boy

   ii a pupil greater than 160cm tall

   iii a girl less than 160cm tall.

b It is known that a pupil selected from Ms Evans tutor group is taller than 1.6 metres. What is the probability that this pupil is a girl?